D0855035

# COALITIONS IN BRITISH POLITICS

*Also by David Butler*

THE BRITISH GENERAL ELECTION OF 1951
THE BRITISH GENERAL ELECTION OF 1955
THE BRITISH GENERAL ELECTION OF 1959 (*with Richard Rose*)
THE BRITISH GENERAL ELECTION OF 1964 (*with Anthony King*)
THE BRITISH GENERAL ELECTION OF 1966 (*with Anthony King*)
THE BRITISH GENERAL ELECTION OF 1970 (*with Michael Pinto-Duschinsky*)
THE BRITISH GENERAL ELECTION OF FEBRUARY 1974 (*with Dennis Kavanagh*)
THE BRITISH GENERAL ELECTION OF OCTOBER 1974 (*with Dennis Kavanagh*)
THE 1975 REFERENDUM (*with Uwe Kitzinger*)
BRITISH POLITICAL FACTS 1900—78 (*5th edition — with Anne Sloman*)
POLITICAL CHANGE IN BRITAIN (*with Donald Stokes*)
THE CANBERRA MODEL

# COALITIONS IN BRITISH POLITICS

Edited by David Butler

*Essays by*
ROBERT BLAKE
KENNETH O. MORGAN
DAVID MARQUAND
A. J. P. TAYLOR
DAVID BUTLER

St. Martin's Press    New York

St. Martin's Press, Inc., 175 Fifth Avenue, New York, N.Y. 10010
Printed in Great Britain
Library of Congress Catalog Card Number 77-17791
ISBN 0-312-14503-9
First published in the United States of America in 1978

Library of Congress Cataloging in Publication Data

Main entry under title:

Coalitions in British politics.

    1. Great Britain—Politics and government—19th century—
Addresses, essays, lectures.   2. Great Britain—Politics
and government—20th century—Addresses, essays, lectures.
3. Coalition governments—Great Britain—Addresses, essays,
lectures.  I. Butler, David E.
JN231.C57     320.9′41′08     77-17791
ISBN 0-312-14503-9

# Contents

# 1 1783–1902

## ROBERT BLAKE

Shortly before 1 a.m. on 17 December 1852, Disraeli in his winding-up speech in defence of an abnormally timed budget, and during a no less abnormally timed thunderstorm, defiantly declared that he was faced by a 'coalition', and he went on:

> The combination may be successful. A Coalition has before this been successful. But Coalitions though successful have always found this, that their triumph has been brief. This too, I know, that England does not love Coalitions.

The words of the last sentence have echoed down the years and have become a part of British political folklore. What did they really mean? Were they simply a statement of distaste at the prospect of the particular combination which was about to overthrow the Tory minority government of Lord Derby, in which Disraeli was Chancellor of the Exchequer and Leader of the House of Commons? Or do they epitomise some profound and general truth about the nature of party politics in Britain? The first coalition of any significance in British political history was the famous or infamous Fox–North Coalition of 1783. The pejorative overtones of the word largely originate from the circumstances of that alliance and no analysis of the concept of coalition is adequate without some reference to it.

The term 'coalition' implies a system in which there are a number of parties competing for political power in an elected legislature. It has little relevance in a period of one-party government of the sort inaugurated by Sir Robert Walpole and ending in the 1760s with the rise of the Rockingham Whigs. There is perhaps some significance in the earliest reference in the Oxford Dictionary to coalition in the political sense of the word. This refers to the title of a book written in 1715 – 'An Essay towards a Coalition of Parties in Great Britain'. There had been throughout the late years of William III and the reign of Queen Anne a fierce party warfare in which contending factions competed bitterly for office. But there followed a period in which party ceased to have much meaning. The Tories became an almost extinct faction. The Whigs acquired a monopoly of patronage and power in which the first two Georges acquiesced. The situation changed when George III reasserted the dormant rights of the monarchy. For ten years the King sought for a prime minister who could manage Parliament satisfactorily on his behalf. It was not till the Duke of Grafton's resignation in 1770 that he succeeded. Lord North was First Lord of the Treasury for the next twelve years.

North was confronted by an opposition party which was divided into two groups. There were the followers of Lord Chatham and the supporters of Lord Rockingham. After Chatham's death in 1778 his mantle fell upon Lord Shelburne, who was upheld by Chatham's youthful political heir, William Pitt the younger. The hereditary mistrust of the house of Fox for that of Pitt might have kept Charles Fox in the ministerialist ranks as a supporter of North, but for the eloquence of Burke and the increasingly disastrous developments in America. Fox could not, however, become a Chathamite. It was to the Rockingham branch of the Whig Opposition that he decided to adhere. For the time being the differences between the two were merged in their determination at all costs to bring down North. With Fox as their leading figure in the House of Commons, they succeeded early in 1782 in forcing North to resign. Fox's eloquent denunciations of Lord North were a major element in achieving this result.

The King accepted an administration headed by Lord Rockingham, with the utmost reluctance. His only consolation was the presence of Lord Shelburne as one of the two Secretaries of State, the other being Fox. Shelburne summed up the situation in a note of subjects discussed at an interview with George III on 21 March 1782. The entries include:

His bad opinion of Lord Rockingham's understanding

His horror of C. Fox

His preference for me compared to the rest of the opposition[1]

It soon became clear that the Whig opposition by defeating Lord North had by no means defeated the King. His powers were not enough to keep a discredited and unpopular administration in office, but they were quite enough to make the existence of a successor government which he disliked extremely uncomfortable. By playing Shelburne off against Rockingham, by creating the impression that it was the Secretary of State, rather than the First Lord of the Treasury who had his ear, the King within three months reduced to a state of demoralised chaos a Whig Party which, in its euphoria at the fall of North, had seen itself as entering the promised land. The heady days when Fox announced to his cronies over the faro table at Brooks's the future dispensation of patronage soon vanished. Even if Rockingham had not died on 1 July, it is unlikely that his government would have lasted much longer. Fox himself, contrary to the later charges of his opponents, was on the verge of resigning in protest at the King's 'unconstitutional' conduct some days before the death of the prime minister. He would have been better placed if he had actually done so. His subsequent resignation when Shelburne became First Lord could too easily be interpreted as the result of personal pique at being passed over, rather than of principle.

The situation in the summer of 1782 – indeed for the next twenty-one months – was not unlike that of 1923–24 or indeed 1977; no party had a clear majority in the House of Commons. There were three groups: the adherents of Lord North, who had governed the country from 1770 till their fall in March; the Chathamite Whigs who were in office with Shelburne at the Treasury and the younger Pitt as Chancellor of the Exchequer; the Rockingham Whigs led, now that their titular head had gone, by Charles James Fox. The great issue before the country was, as it had been for twenty years, America – the specific problem now being the conditions of peace. On America Lord North felt highly vulnerable. The possibility of proscription and impeachment as a result of the disasters during his premiership was seldom far from his mind. Impeachment had not yet become a rusty weapon. It was to be used against Warren Hastings and later against Dundas, though both men were in the end acquitted. North did not feel safe in opposition. Politically he was in many respects nearer to Shelburne than Fox. The snag about joining the government was that Pitt, in accordance with family tradition, regarded North with the deepest disapproval. No administration could hold them both, and Shelburne could not dispense with Pitt.

An alliance between Fox and Shelburne was equally impossible for a similar reason. After his experience in Rockingham's Cabinet, Fox was convinced that Shelburne was a double-faced minion of the King, and that he played a role which was contrary to the whole spirit if not the letter of the constitution. If Fox was to obtain office he could only do so by a junction with North. If North was to secure immunity from impeachment he could only do so by an alliance with Fox. There was, however, one difficulty. No man in the run-up to the fall of North's ministry had denounced the prime minister with greater invective than Fox. Moreover on the crucial issue of royal power and constitutional reform Fox, in terms of the doctrinal spectrum of the time, was at the opposite end to North, whereas Shelburne was somewhere in the middle.

It took some time before the problem of reconciliation could be solved, but North was good-natured to a fault, and Fox had convinced himself that there was no other way to curb what he regarded as the encroachment of the executive upon the sphere of Parliament. He rightly reckoned that in any coalition with North his own would be the dominant voice. Early in 1783 the two opposites came together and narrowly defeated Shelburne's peace proposals after what George III called 'the extraordinary and never-to-be-forgot vote of February 1783'. For six weeks he tried to fend off its consequences, but eventually succumbed. The Duke of Portland became titular First Lord of the Treasury with Fox and North as Secretaries of State.

The Coalition fell in December. It was destroyed by the King, and the verdict of contemporaries and historians has been on his side. Undoubtedly it was a failure by any of the tests of success which might be applied to a government then or now. It lasted for only eight months. It solved no major problems. Its very existence scandalised a large part of the political nation and it fell on an issue which scandalised an even larger part – a Bill which would have vested the patronage of the East India Company in the hands of Fox's friends and which as a result of the electoral influence thus gained seemed likely to perpetuate their power in Britain. The 'unconstitutionality' of the King's conduct in putting pressure on the peers to throw it out became blurred by the dubious nature of the measure rejected. These events bequeathed a legacy of discredit to the very word 'coalition' – a legacy which has increased at compound interest ever since.

It was no doubt the Fox–North Coalition which Disraeli had in mind when he used his famous words in 1852. Indeed it is difficult to see what else he could have meant if coalition is defined as an alliance between two or more hitherto separate or even hostile groups or parties formed in order to carry on the government and share the principal offices of state. Between 1783 and 1852 numerous governments of a rather hybrid nature held office: the younger Pitt's administration after the junction with the Portland Whigs in 1794; the 'Ministry of All the Talents', 1806–7; Liverpool's government after the adherence of the Grenvillites in 1822; Canning's short-lived Cabinet of 1827 with four Whig members. None of these are quite comparable to the Fox–North Coalition, nor was the word used in reference to them. The junction of the Portland Whigs with Pitt is the nearest equivalent, but Portland only brought a portion of the Whig party with him. The special feature of the Fox–North Coalition was that the two leaders had behind them the overwhelming majority of the previously hostile parties which they led. It was not a matter of individuals or groups seceding piecemeal from the main body. Another feature which distinguished it from the alliance between Pitt and Portland, and also from the Asquith, the first Lloyd George, and the Churchill coalitions of the twentieth century was that it did not stem from the necessities of war which might naturally be supposed to produce some sort of government of national unity. It was a peacetime expedient.

Disraeli, contemplating the political prospect before him in the small hours of 17 December 1852, correctly foresaw that Derby's minority administration would fall and be succeeded by a coalition. This was not an inevitable outcome. It is true that ever since 1846 the House had been divided three ways and no single party had had a clear majority. This of course had been the situation in 1782–3 and it was one which was likely to make men think of a coalition. But there was an alternative in the form of a minority government preserving power by a pact, explicit or unavowed, with one of the other parties. An explicit pact came into being in 1977 between Labour and Liberal. A similar pact with the Liberal Unionists sustained Lord Salisbury from 1886 to 1892. After Peel's resignation in 1846, the Conservative party divided into two groups, Protectionists and Peelites. The general election of 1847 gave the former 243 seats and the latter 89, while the Whigs and their allies amounted to 324 – a minority of eight against the other two parties combined. But no coalition ensued. Peel was highly averse to office, and it was quite feasible in those days to carry on a minority government for several years. Peel did not enter into any explicit pact with Lord John Russell, but it was known that he would do almost anything to keep the Protectionists out. This unavowed agreement maintained Russell in office till early in 1852 when he fell on a snap vote engineered by Palmerston, who had been dismissed the year before and sought his revenge.

Lord Derby took office at the head of another minority government and dissolved parliament in the summer. The result was similar to 1846. No party had a clear majority. The Protectionists rose to 290, the Peelites fell to 45 and the Whigs stayed much the same at 319. Derby resigned as soon as he had been defeated on the budget, and within a few days the celebrated Aberdeen Coalition had been formed.

The moral justification for this combination was said by some people to be the ambiguous attitude of the Derbyites on the question of fiscal policy. At the general election in the summer of 1852 they were described as protectionists in the counties, free traders in the big boroughs and neutral in the small ones. The argument was not in itself very powerful. Long before the fall of Derby's government it was perfectly obvious that the Tories had no intention of reintroducing the corn laws, and indeed they had accepted a resolution to that effect in November even before Disraeli introduced his budget.[2] It was on the strength of this acceptance that the Peelites took no immediate steps to eject the government, but preferred to wait and see what emerged from the budget, anticipating that it would probably provide them with good grounds for opposition.

The issue which brought matters to a head was the 'differentiation' of the income tax. 'Differentiation' in the jargon of the day meant the distinction between 'precarious' and 'realised' incomes. The modern equivalent would roughly be the different way in which earned and unearned incomes are treated. Disraeli proposed in his budget to tax 'precarious' incomes at three-quarters of the rate of 'realised' incomes.

Unfortunately he equated this distinction with the income tax
schedules, although these did not in fact correspond to it at all closely.
For example Disraeli left Schedule A (incomes derived from land) at
the full rate. Yet, as his critics pointed out, Schedule A also included
incomes derived from businesses connected with the land — collieries,
quarries etc. – which were indistinguishable from the general run of
incomes under Schedule D (profits from trade, businesses,
professions), which were to be charged at the lower rate. There were
several similar illogicalities. The result was that, quite apart from the
general question of making such a differential at all, which was in itself
highly controversial, Disraeli could be convicted of slapdash muddle
even in terms of achieving his own objectives. No one felt more strongly
on this than Gladstone and it was he who brought the Derby/Disraeli
government to an end, and at the same time brought the Peelites down
from the fence on which they had been sitting for the last six years.

His memorandum on the matter which he read to Lord Aberdeen on
the afternoon of 18 December 1852 is explicit on the justification of a
coalition. Observing that neither a purely Liberal or purely
Conservative government was now feasible, he argued for what he
called a 'mixed government'.

> The formation of a mixed Government can only be warrantable or
> auspicious when its members have the most thorough confidence in
> the honour, integrity and fidelity of each other: when they are agreed
> in principle upon all the great questions of public policy immediately
> emergent: and lastly when a great and palpable emergency of state
> calls for such a formation.
>
> Such an exigency exists at the present moment and not only with
> respect to contingencies which may happen in connection with our
> foreign affairs: but more visibly and immediately with regard to a
> subject on which the public mind is always accessible, ready and re-
> ceptive; with reference, namely, to finance.[3]

Gladstone went on to observe that income tax had always been levied
from all classes of income equally, but that there had been a revulsion
against this principle:

> Stimulated by the public journals this revulsion has hitherto been
> borne down only by the firm union and combination, continued for a
> half century, of political authorities: all persons who are responsible
> for the Government of the country having, whether on the same or
> different grounds, agreed in charging the tax equally on all incomes.
>
> But now an Executive Government has promulgated the principle
> that a distinction is to be drawn between realised and precarious

incomes . . .

This amounts to a proclamation to all classes that their relative
position is to be changed: an invitation to them to enter into conflict
upon the terms of that change: an assurance from the Executive
Government to a large part of them that they are unjustly taxed and a
distinct encouragement to resist the continuance of such taxation.

He went on to express the fear that the income tax and the whole
financial system were thus placed in jeopardy and that there is 'a
resistless call' for the matter to be settled.

All the strength that can be brought to the task may prove
inadequate; none of it can be superfluous.

And further, is it not in the most temperate portion of both the
Conservative and Liberal parties, that support for such an effort is
chiefly to be sought?

Thus then the third condition of a mixed Government is realised.
As to the two former, I assume and I thoroughly believe in their
existence.

By a mixed Government I mean something different from a fusion
of parties. A mixed Government may be honourably formed, but a
fusion of parties could not, with a reserve upon political questions
more remotely impending, such as that upon Parliamentary Reform:
a reserve to this extent, that upon all the particulars and details of such
a measure, which must in reality, determine its sense and spirit, every
man will retain an entire freedom.

The formation of the coalition was a laborious process. The final
result owed much to the support of the Crown. Prince Albert was a
natural Peelite.[4] On submitting his resignation at Osborne on 17
December, Derby advised the Queen to send for Lord Lansdowne. The
latter was the Nestor of the Whig party and had actually served as
Chancellor of the Exchequer in the 'Ministry of All the Talents' forty-
six years earlier. Derby said that he had heard that a Whig–Peelite
combination might be formed under Lord Aberdeen, but he thought it
better for the Queen to see Lansdowne first 'who knew better than
anyone the state of the Parties and would give the best advice'. He did
not, he said, advise that Aberdeen should be sent for yet, since if it were
reported that he had given such advice many Conservatives, in view of
his (Derby's) declaration that he would retire from public life in the
event of defeat, would think it necessary to join Aberdeen. The
remainder who bitterly resented the Peelite attack on the budget would
take factious vengeance on the Government and 'the great Conservative
Party would be broken up, which it was so essential for the country to
keep together and moderate'.[5] Prince Albert commented that strictly it

was not for Derby to give advice. Derby agreed, but observed that it was often said, e.g., that 'Lord John Russell advised the Queen to send for Lord Derby'. He added, 'rather jokingly', that the Cabinet could not number less than thirty-two if all the claims of ex-ministers were to be met.

In the event the Queen and the Prince decided to summon Lansdowne and Aberdeen simultaneously, but Lansdowne was laid low by gout, and so Aberdeen came on his own after consulting Lansdowne who made it clear that he was most reluctant to assume the premiership. Lansdowne's virtual refusal meant that the Coalition, despite the overwhelming predominance of the Whigs and Radicals (according to Lord John Russell, 270) over the Peelites (according to the same authority, only 30) would be headed by a Peelite. Lord John was generally regarded as impossible and the Peelites would not have served under him, though they were ready to serve with him.[6] Palmerston was in an isolated position and gravely discredited. As with Churchill in 1940 it needed a war – and one that was going extremely badly – to bring him to the highest office, but even in 1852 he was sufficiently influential for his open declaration that he would never serve under Russell to make the latter's candidature impossible. There was no other Whig who could be regarded as *papabile*. Lansdowne suggested to the Queen that she should ask Aberdeen and Russell to arrange jointly the distribution of offices, but Aberdeen was pressed strongly by Sir James Graham, a prominent Peelite, to insist on sole responsibility and he agreed to do so.

There was endless trouble about the position of Lord John Russell. As the last Whig prime minister, as author of the Reform Act of 1832, as a younger son of one of the greatest Whig dynasties, he possessed, despite his oddities, his eccentricities and his tiresome second wife, a prestige which made him an indispensable member of the Coalition. But he was thin-skinned, sensitive about his loss of status, and fussy about his 'honour'. Aberdeen offered him the Foreign Office and the leadership of the House of Commons. At first he said yes. Then he said that the burden of the Foreign Office would be too much: he would rather stay out of office and give 'independent support'. He was pressed to take the leadership in combination with some nominal office. But no such office seemed compatible with his dignity. The Lord Presidency was erroneously believed at the time to be a post confined to the House of Lords. The only alternative, the Chancellorship of the Duchy of Lancaster, Russell considered to be too low. Would it be possible to lead the House with a seat in Cabinet, but no paid office? This was alleged by some to be unconstitutional on the ground that Russell would evade the usual by-election which followed acceptance of a position in the Government. Russell offered to apply for the Chiltern Hundreds and fight for re-election. Sir James Graham argued that a minister without office deriving his authority exclusively from the House might 'become almost a dictator'. Gladstone on the other hand argued that he would not carry enough weight.

In the end an agreement which boded ill for the future was achieved. Russell took on the Foreign Office along with the leadership of the House on the understanding that he would relinquish the former in favour of Lord Clarendon as soon as he found it too much for his health, which he predicted, with remarkable lack of doubt, would be in February 1853 when the new session began. There was also an under-standing – or so Lord John believed, although there is some doubt about it – that Aberdeen would vacate the premiership in his favour as soon as the allegedly temporary objections to Russell's appointment had evaporated.[7] It is surprising that any of the other parties concerned should have agreed with these arrangements.

Aberdeen, who is often depicted as a weak and vacillating prime minister, was very firm when he came to deal with the composition of the rest of the Cabinet and the filling of minor offices. The Cabinet consisted of six Peelites, six Whigs and one Radical. The Peelites held not only the premiership, but the posts of Chancellor of the Exchequer (Gladstone) and – of greater significance in view of the Crimean War than could have been foreseen at the time – those of Secretary for War and Colonies (Duke of Newcastle), First Lord of the Admiralty (Graham), and Secretary at War (Sidney Herbert). The majority of ministerial appointments outside the Cabinet went to Whigs or Liberals, though one of the most important, the Board of Trade, was given to Edward Cardwell, a Peelite. Of the non-Peelites in the Cabinet only three active orthodox regular Whigs were included – Russell, Granville (President of the Council) and Sir Charles Wood (President of the Board of Control). Of the others, Palmerston (Home Secretary) had been dismissed from the last Whig government; Cranworth (the Lord Chancellor) was virtually non-political, Lord Lansdowne, who was in the Cabinet but took no office, had almost retired from public life and Sir William Molesworth (First Commissioner of Works), who was the only Radical, had never sat in a Cabinet at all.[8]

Yet as Professor Conacher points out,[9] the two previous governments, Russell's and Derby's, 'had been defeated by the votes of independent Liberals and independent Conservatives'. It was not unreasonable to think that party lines needed to be redrawn and that a government constructed on the lines of Aberdeen's

> would obtain support not only from the Liberal Conservatives who voted against the Disraeli budget but also from quite a few more followers of Lord Derby who would be ready, after Lord Derby's failure to give fair trial to an administration headed by a former Con-servative Foreign Secretary and containing six former Conservative

ministers. To have included a predominant number of Liberal
ministers in the Cabinet would have been to close the ranks of the
Conservatives behind Lord Derby.

The Aberdeen Coalition does not go down to history as a success. It has
had a bad press from historians and politicians. It lasted little over two
years and, as Gladstone observed, the majority against it 'not only
knocked us down, but sent us down with such a thwack that one heard
one's head thump as it hit the ground'. The question is whether
Aberdeen's government collapsed because of its nature as a coalition
between two parties or whether it collapsed through circumstances
which would equally have brought about the fall of a homogeneous
administration.

It must be said that, whatever its defects, the Coalition did manage to
achieve its immediate purpose. The situation in the House may not
strictly have necessitated a 'mixed Government' but without some such
arrangement there was a vista of indefinite instability. Derby's
resignation as a result of the Peelite attack on Disraeli's budget meant
that no reunion of Conservatives could take place in the near future. Sir
Stafford Northcote was surely barking up the wrong tree when he wrote
to Gladstone urging the Peelites 'to assert themselves as a purely
Conservative Administration, claiming the support of the whole
Conservative body and that alone', especially when he added that they
should rest their claim 'to supersede Lord Derby on the simple ground
of their superior capacity for administering the financial and other
affairs of the country'.[10] The snag in this argument was that, despite the
famous joke about the 'Who?, Who?' Ministry, despite the undoubted
mediocrity or inexperience of Derby's Cabinet of 1852, apart from
Derby himself ('he *is* the Government', Queen Victoria wrote), and
despite Disraeli's ill-prepared budget, the rank and file of the Conservative party were simply not prepared to accept the leadership of a set of
men, however able and high-minded, who had recently rubbed their
noses in the dirt and ejected them from office.

If there was to be any combination which could command a majority
in the House it had to be some sort of Whig—Peelite alliance. And on
what Gladstone regarded as the 'great and palpable emergency' which
demanded such a coalition, i.e. the differentiation of the income tax, no
alliance with Disraeli was possible, quite apart from personal
antipathies, although these were powerful enough in themselves. Moreover, Gladstone's great budget of 1853 did in fact deal with this
emergency. It may seem ironical today that the future leader of the
Liberal party should have nailed his colours to the mast of non-
differentiation between earned and unearned income, whereas the
future leader of the Conservatives tried to make the distinction. For
good or ill, Gladstone succeeded and it was not till over half a century

had elapsed, in fact in Asquith's budget of 1907, that an attempt was again made, this time successfully, to tax 'precarious' at a lower rate than 'realised' incomes. In this and many other respects Gladstone's first budget as Chancellor of the Exchequer in the Aberdeen Coalition established the financial orthodoxies followed by all political parties for the rest of the nineteenth century.

The first year of the Coalition was successful. Russell duly found the Foreign Office too much for him in February 1853 and ceded it to Clarendon, while retaining the leadership of the House and membership of the Cabinet without office. On the whole he was reasonably co-operative and his only offer of resignation was not very serious. Palmerston proved to be remarkably enterprising at the Home Office and introduced important reforms in the field of what would now be called environmental pollution. In the three areas where *The Times* in March 1853 declared that great questions needed to be settled, income tax, India and national education, the Coalition could fairly claim to have coped with the first in Gladstone's budget and the second in the India Act of 1853. Education, however, foundered, as so often before and after, on the rock of religious bigotry, and the Education Bill of 1853 sank without trace.

It cannot be said that Aberdeen was a powerful or dominant prime minister. He was an indifferent speaker and perhaps suffered from being one of the only two holders of his office since the Duke of Portland who never sat in the House of Commons (Lord Rosebery was the other). His taciturnity and inability to communicate in debate was, however, balanced by a combination of honesty, fair dealing and conciliatoriness in Cabinet, which greatly helped to smooth over the difficulties inherent in a mixed government. Despite his rather dour and bleak exterior he gained the respect and affection of his close colleagues. 'He is the man in public life of all others whom I have *loved*', Gladstone told his granddaughter-in-law long afterwards.[11] It says much for Aberdeen that Palmerston, of whose foreign policy he had been one of the sharpest critics, was prepared to serve under him. True, they had been at Harrow together as boys nearly sixty years earlier, but that was no guarantee of harmony in itself, and Palmerston in 1849 had referred to him (not actually by name, but everyone knew who was meant) as an example of 'antiquated imbecility'.

Aberdeen had two other assets, one of which reflected his personality, the other being sheer luck. He got on better with the Queen and the Prince than almost any other prime minister during their time. Unlike Russell he kept her fully informed of everything that was going on and was invariably courteous and considerate. A common love for Aberdeenshire may have helped. Unlike Derby, who was certainly more communicative than Russell, he did not have what Palmerston called 'an off-hand and sarcastic manner', nor would he have dreamed of presenting her, as Derby did, with a list of Household appointments of whom the Prince noted with horror 'the greater part were the Dandies and Roués of London and the Turf'.[12]

His other asset was adventitious. Although the Coalition could only just outvote the Derbyites if they turned up in strength and could be beaten if the Radicals and the 'Irish Brigade' joined in, the opposition was in a state of discredit and confusion. Disraeli was extremely unpopular. Derby was on the worst terms that he was to be at any time with his second-in-command, and the party was in a general state of disarray which was not improved by a series of scandals about the late general election, dragged up during the course of the year. The Whigs and Peelites were not, of course, immune from similar charges, but the Derbyites came out much worse and were particularly damaged by revelations about one of the Carlton Club agents, a certain Mr Frail, whose name caused great merriment in governmental quarters. On one occasion as many as a hundred Derbyites voted with the Government and on more than one occasion over fifty.[13]

What wrecked the Coalition was the Eastern Question and the Crimean War. The subject is one of immense complication and cannot be recounted here even in outline. It is generally agreed by historians that the war was 'unnecessary', and that it could have been averted either if Aberdeen had had his way or, less certainly, if Palmerston, Russell and Lansdowne had had their way. Aberdeen would have insisted on the Turks accepting the 'Vienna Note'. This had been agreed by the Czar and it would have been a satisfactory settlement of the religious question on which the whole issue turned. The Whig trio on the other hand would have made it clear from the beginning that Britain was ready to go to war in defence of Turkey against Russia. This approach might or might not have worked, but it would at least have prevented the Czar putting himself into a position from which he could not discover an honourable retreat. The conflicts in the Cabinet between these opposing views produced a compromise which, whatever its theoretical merits, did in fact lead to war.

War has twice in modern times led to coalition, but in this case an existing coalition collapsed because of war. The administration which saw out the Crimean War was to be a Whig/Liberal government under Palmerston. The question which any historical analysis of coalitions must raise is whether the entry into war, the disasters of war and the defeat of the Government occurred because it was a coalition. Or would something of the sort have happened even under a politically homogeneous Cabinet? To these three separate questions there can be no certain answers. One can only speculate.

It is clear that the divisions within the Cabinet about the attitude towards the Vienna Note corresponded to a certain degree with party distinctions. The anti-Russian trio were Whigs, later reinforced by the

Foreign Secretary, Clarendon, who was also a Whig. Aberdeen's more pacific line at first had the backing of Gladstone, Graham, Argyll and Herbert – all Peelites. There were cross-currents. Wood and Granville were at that stage in the peace party and so was Clarendon. The Duke of Newcastle moved into the anti-Russian group. If Russell, Lansdowne or Palmerston had headed a purely Whig Cabinet, a hard line against Russia would have been taken. If Aberdeen had headed a purely Conservative administration the pacific line would have prevailed. In the event drift and confusion and obscurity resulted in war. To that extent it can be argued that the Crimean War *might* have been – though no one can be sure that it *would* have been – averted if there had been no coalition. It is fair to add that all members of the Cabinet assumed responsibility, and both Gladstone and Argyll, who belonged to the peace party, went out of their way to defend the Cabinet's policy subsequently in print.

The second question is the conduct of the war. The disasters which occurred need no recapitulation, but it is not at all obvious that they had a connection with the fact that the government was a coalition. Any government would have inherited a legacy of unpreparedness, sloth, red tape, bureaucracy and general ineptitude. Any government would have been damaged by the publicity given to the horrors of war by new developments in what would now be called the media. Before the Coalition fell most of the really serious defects in the military machine were on the way to being repaired. Although Palmerston came in as the man of the moment after Aberdeen resigned, there is little evidence that he contributed to the efficient conduct of the war, and some to suggest that he contributed to its unnecessary prolongation.

As for the defeat of the Government, it is on the other hand a reasonable assumption that its nature as a coalition was a major cause. But this was largely due to the personality of Lord John Russell. He evidently at heart never understood why he had to step down from the top position in politics. He was also convinced that Aberdeen had gone back on a bargain to retire in his favour. After the first year of the Coalition he behaved with increasing irresponsibility, making continuous threats of resignation on issues some of which were trivial. His conduct at the end cannot be defended. He resigned because he could not, so he said, vote against a committee of inquiry into the conduct of the war. This was a fatal blow and, although the motion might have been carried anyway, the defection of Russell would have occurred sooner or later and would have brought the Coalition to an end. If there is any moral to be drawn, it is that a coalition cannot survive if the man who leads the largest number of its supporters is a vain and prickly *prima donna* occupying the second place while convinced that he ought to have the first.

The Coalition did not quite come to its end with Aberdeen's

resignation. After first Derby, then Lansdowne, and finally Russell had decided that it was impossible for them to form a government, the Queen sent for Palmerston, who re-created the Coalition minus Aberdeen and Newcastle. The latter felt too sensitive to remain, on account of the largely unjustified attacks upon him over the conduct of the war. Aberdeen was strongly pressed by Prince Albert, but in a letter to Sidney Herbert of which he forwarded a copy to the Prince he said,

> If at any future time my presence should be required in a Cabinet, I should feel no objection to accept any office, or to enter it without office. But to be the Head of a Cabinet today, and to become a subordinate member of the very same Cabinet tomorrow, would be a degradation to which I could never submit. I would rather die than do so.[14]

The five[15] remaining Peelites, after first refusing, decided to accept office, but barely a fortnight later Gladstone, Graham and Herbert resigned on the ground that the government ought not to have acquiesced in the motion to nominate the members of the committee demanded by Roebuck. Since the Aberdeen government had fallen by being heavily defeated on the question whether there should be such a committee at all, it seems odd that the three Peelites should have chosen the mere nomination of the committee as a resigning matter; they might well have declined to accept Palmerston's offer, but having done so they were open to serious criticism for straining at the gnat of the actual nomination.[16] Argyll and Canning remained in office, but the administration lost its coalition character from then onwards.

The Aberdeen Cabinet, though it was in Gladstone's terminology a 'mixed' government, led in the end to a 'fusion of parties'. The Peelites, partly because of their experience in co-operation with the Whigs, partly because of the consequential widening of the gap between the two Conservative groups, partly because of personal antipathies (Disraeli being high on the list), moved into the Whig orbit. Gladstone took the vital decision in 1859 when, after paradoxically voting against the successful amendment moved by the Whigs to Derby's Address in reply to the Queen's Speech, he accepted Palmerston's offer of the Chancellorship of the Exchequer. Four other Peelites also joined (Argyll, Herbert, Newcastle and Cardwell). This is as good a date as any at which to fix the birth of the Liberal Party – an amalgamation of Whigs, Peelites and Radicals, which was to be in office for rather more than half the remaining years of the nineteenth century.

The effect of this union was to clarify the party composition of the House of Commons. Electoral verdicts became even more definitive with the passing of the Reform Act of 1867. The elections of 1868, 1874, 1880 and 1885 produced unambiguous results, i.e. a clear victory for the

Liberals (three) or the Conservatives (one). It is true that those of 1857 and 1865 appeared to do the same, but the fluidity of party politics was such that in both cases parliament ejected the winner before the next election took place. Between 1841 and 1865 there was only one parliament (that of 1859) which did not subsequently turn out the government that had won the election. A coalition situation did not arise for more than thirty years after Aberdeen's resignation.

The development which transformed the scene was a combination of the increased strength of the Irish Nationalists as a result of the Reform Act of 1884 and Gladstone's decision late in 1885, to make Home Rule for Ireland – 'devolution', it would be called to-day – the principal plank of the Liberal platform. Gladstone had resigned as a result of defeat on a snap vote in June 1885, and Lord Salisbury headed a minority Conservative government which could not dissolve till late in the autumn when the new electoral register would be ready. The general election produced a clear victory in one sense for the Liberals – 335 as against 249 Conservatives. But Parnell won 86 seats. He was thus in a position to keep either party out of power, but only the Liberals in. Gladstone, contrary to the allegations of his enemies, had become a convert to Home Rule before the election. His silence hitherto on the subject stemmed from his hope that the Conservatives might bring forward such a measure, which would have a far better chance of enactment under their auspices than under his. In reality, though Gladstone could not know this, Salisbury too had already made up his mind before the full results were out. The Conservatives in his view could have no truck with Home Rule, and he wrote to the Queen's private secretary to that effect on 29 November.[17]

Gladstone's views were prematurely revealed to the press by an indiscretion of his son Herbert on 17 December, and from that moment onwards the battle lines were drawn. The 'Hawarden Kite', as Herbert Gladstone's revelation was called with singular injustice, removed any lingering chance there might have been of the Tory Cabinet reconsidering the question. The only home ruler in it, the Irish Viceroy, Lord Carnarvon, resigned. Salisbury announced his intention of bringing in a Coercion Act as soon as possible after parliament reassembled, and on 26 January 1886 the Liberals and the Irish combined to defeat the government on an amendment to the Address. It was significant that 18 Liberals voted with the government and no less than 74 abstained.

When Gladstone formed his Cabinet, the principal figures among the Whig element of the party headed by Lord Hartington declined to join. This might have been expected. Hartington, son of the Duke of Devonshire and representative of one of the greatest Whig dynasties, had long been in sentiment much nearer to Salisbury than to Gladstone, and the same could be said of many of his followers who adhered to the Liberal party more from tradition than conviction. What was much less predictable was the attitude of the Radical element. Most of them stood by Gladstone, but a section headed by Joseph Chamberlain was as hostile to Home Rule as the Whigs were. Both Chamberlain and Sir George Trevelyan, however, accepted office.

Chamberlain's motives are not clear. He was profoundly antipathetic to an Irish parliament, but it has to be remembered that in theory Gladstone was only committed to an 'inquiry' into the Irish question with the object of ascertaining whether and how the demands of the Parnellites could be met. Chamberlain may have hoped to influence the nature of the plan in the course of Cabinet discussions.[18] If so he was to be disappointed. Early in March Gladstone announced to the Cabinet his firm proposals for an Irish parliament, and by the end of the month both Chamberlain and Trevelyan had resigned. The Home Rule Bill duly went forward, but was thrown out on the second reading on 7 June, by 343 votes to 313. No less than 93 Liberals voted with the majority. Gladstone promptly dissolved parliament. The ensuing election was an emphatic repudiation of Home Rule by the non-Irish parts of the United Kingdom. The Parnellite strength remained the same, but the Liberals fell from 335 to 191, the Conservatives rose from 249 to 316, and the dissident Liberals soon to be christened 'Liberal Unionists', held the balance with 78 seats. During the election there was a bargain, not always observed, between Conservatives and Liberal Unionists not to split the anti-Gladstonian vote.

The obvious answer in such a situation was a coalition between the Conservatives and the dissentient Liberals. Although it was not at all clear that the top position should go to a Liberal Unionist, Salisbury offered to serve under Hartington if the latter was willing to become prime minister of such an alliance. He refused. It is a curious fact that even the Whig section of the Liberal Unionists was very reluctant to join with the Tories. A similar aversion had been displayed earlier during the run-up to the defeat of the Home Rule Bill, and the experiment of Whigs and Tories appearing on the same platform, which took place on 14 April was not repeated. 'Their view', Salisbury wrote to a friend, 'seems to be that in allying themselves with us they are contracting a mésalliance; and though they are affectionate in private they don't like showing us to their friends till they have had time to prepare them for the shock'.[19]

Hartington's motive was not as trivial as this. The Liberal Unionists comprised two groups of M.P.s who had hitherto been deeply opposed to each other in almost every issue. It was a great testimony to Gladstone's prestige and skill that the Liberal Cabinet of 1880 to 1885 had been kept together at all. The Hartingtonians and the Chamberlainites from the early months of 1886 were united on one point – and one only; they were determined to block Home Rule. On all the social and other measures which Chamberlain had propounded in

his 'Unauthorised Programme' of 1885 there was a profound gap
between the two factions. If, therefore, Irish Home Rule was to be the
vital question, Gladstone's point in reference to the Aberdeen Coalition
worked the other way. There was indeed 'a great and palpable
emergency of state',[20] but Hartington could not be sure of keeping the
Whig Unionists and the Radical Unionists together on this question if
he took office. It was regarded then as inconceivable that Chamberlain
could join a Liberal Unionist/Conservative coalition, and the result of
Hartington's participation, whether as head or simply a member, would
mean that 'Chamberlain would be left with so small a following that he
would have no choice but to slide back into Gladstonianism'.[21]

Hartington had a valid point. Chamberlain's position was isolated
and dangerous. Of the 78 Liberal Unionists only 21 were
Chamberlainites according to the calculations of the Conservative chief
whip, Akers Douglas.[22] Chamberlain was further weakened when his
one potential ally in the Conservative Cabinet, Lord Randolph
Churchill, committed political suicide at the end of 1886. He was
replaced by Goschen, a Liberal Unionist of the Right if ever there was
one – an ominous sign, although Hartington still remained aloof.
Chamberlain did at this stage make some sort of effort to return to the
old Liberal fold, but the 'Round Table' Conference of 1887, designed to
reunite the Radical Unionists, and ultimately the Whig Unionists too,
with Gladstone, ended without agreement. From then onwards
Chamberlain moved inexorably away from his old party.

There was no coalition during the 1886–92 parliament, but the
Liberal Unionists of both brands gave systematic support to Salisbury,
and the Chamberlainites had the pleasure of seeing a number of their
own cherished policies enacted, including the reform of local government, the extension of free elementary education and various measures
about allotments and smallholdings. It is arguable whether all or any of
these measures were in fact the result of the balance of power held by the
Liberal Unionists. It is quite possible that the Conservatives would have
brought them in anyway, but they provided the Liberal Unionists,
especially the Radical section, with a justification for their informal
pact with Salisbury. Chamberlain wrote to Dr Dale on 1 May 1891:

I have in the last five years seen more progress made with the
practical application of my political programme than in all my
previous life. I owe this result entirely to my former opponents, and
all the opposition has come from my former friends. I am bound to
bear this in mind in my future speeches.[23]

In December of that year, on his father's death, Hartington succeeded as
Duke of Devonshire. It was a sign of how much the gap between Whig
and Radical Unionists had been narrowed that Chamberlain became

their leader in the House of Commons. The general election of 1892 resulted in a narrow victory for Gladstone, whose supporters with the addition of 81 Irish Nationalists had a majority over the Unionists of only 40. The Liberal Unionists fell from 78 to 47. No one expected the government to last for long, nor did it. But inevitably Home Rule was again the central issue in politics and this was bound to consolidate the Unionist alliance. The second Home Rule Bill was carried in the House of Commons, but was rejected by the Lords in 1893. Gladstone resigned early in 1894 to be succeeded by Lord Rosebery, temperamentally perhaps the least well suited holder of the office since Goderich. He resigned after defeat on a snap vote in June 1895, and Salisbury formed his new government in anticipation of an immediate general election.

For many months it had been generally assumed that the leading Liberal Unionists would be included. Time had softened past antagonisms and the prospect of any reconciliation with the old Liberal party had become remote. Nevertheless Chamberlain was anxious to preserve the Liberal Unionists as a separate party and clear that any coalition would be on very specific terms. In October 1894 he presented Salisbury with a 'Memorandum of a Programme of Social Reform' and suggested that a clutch of such measures might be introduced in the House of Lords and sent down to the Commons with highly embarrassing implications for the government. Salisbury replied in terms of partial though by no means total acceptance, but it was evident that an offer would be made to include the Liberal Unionists.

Rosebery's defeat occurred on 21 June. Two days of acrimonious debate in the Cabinet ensued. The question was whether to resign or dissolve. The decision for resignation which the Queen rather surprisingly regarded as 'unconstitutional' was essentially Rosebery's. On 24 June Salisbury was sent for. He decided to form a government and dissolve as soon as possible. Along with Balfour who led the Conservatives in the Commons he conferred with the Duke of Devonshire and Chamberlain about the allocation of offices. It was to be a Coalition government, and in a Cabinet of nineteen there were five Liberal Unionists. At the moment of dissolution the strength of the Liberal Unionists was between one-fifth and one-sixth of the number of Conservative MPs. The fact that they had over a quarter of the Cabinet caused adverse comment in some Tory circles, but two points have to be remembered. It was not known then whether the general election would give the Liberal Unionists the balance of power as the Peelites had had in 1852 or they themselves in 1886. In any case, even if they were to be in that position they would have nothing like the share which Aberdeen secured for his followers.

In fact, of course, the calculation did not proceed on these lines. In obtaining the adherence of the Duke of Devonshire Salisbury was gaining one of the weightiest and most respected figures in a still partly deferential country, and in that of Joseph Chamberlain, the foremost debater in the Commons, a platform orator of great power, and one of the most galvanic personalities of the day with an appeal to just that radical part of the Unionist electorate least likely to be attracted by the Duke. These were considerations which far outweighed numerical balances. The real elements in the political mixture were to be seen when Salisbury offered the Foreign Office to the Duke and any office he wished, apart from the Foreign Office, to Chamberlain. In the event the Duke preferred to be Lord President, and Salisbury, as he had in the past, doubled the Foreign Office with the Premiership. Rather surprisingly, as it seemed at the time, Chamberlain chose the Colonial Office. The other Liberal Unionists were Goschen at the Admiralty, Lansdowne at the War Office and Lord James of Hereford, who had a claim to the Lord Chancellorship[24] but reluctantly took office as Chancellor of the Duchy of Lancaster with a seat in the Cabinet.

The election took place in mid-July after a short campaign and was by way of being a Unionist landslide. The final results gave the Conservatives 341 seats and the Liberal Unionists 70. The Liberal score was 177 and the Irish Nationalist 82. So the Liberal Unionists did not in the event hold the balance. The Conservatives unaided could just out-vote all the other groups added together. With the support of the Liberal Unionists they had a majority of 152. In the aftermath of the general election the proposal of fusion was again mooted, but Chamberlain continued to be convinced that the causes for which he stood would be jeopardised. The Liberal Unionists accordingly retained their own Whips, their own fund and their own party machine. That there was not more friction between them and the Conservatives was largely due to excellent personal relations between Balfour and Chamberlain, springing from the need to concert opposition to the late government and subsequently cemented by co-operation in office.

Chamberlain's tenure of the Colonial Office was memorable and controversial. It lasted for eight years and was filled with notable events, but it did not in itself raise any special problems for the government *qua* coalition. The most which can be said is that Chamberlain may have chosen it partly because it offered particular opportunities to a minister who more than any other Liberal Unionist was an outsider. He would not, in pursuing his well-thought-out plans as head of one of the most torpid departments of state, be cutting across positive accepted orthodoxies, if only because there were none. He could take a strong idiosyncratic line without ruffling the party sentiments either of Tories or of his own brand of radicals. He would, of course, offend the Gladstonians and Little Englanders, but he did not worry about doing that.

The Coalition sailed on through the storms of the Jameson Raid and the South African War. It was lucky to win the 'Khaki' election of

October 1900 – the first time a Cabinet has dissolved with the deliberate object of cashing in on a particular situation. Britain appeared to have won the war, though in the event it was to linger on for nearly two years, and this seemed an opportune moment to exploit patriotic sentiment. It was a shrewd move in terms of party advantage. A year later the Unionists would have fared much worse. But the result was to put the Coalition in a basically false position. A 'patriotic mandate' did not necessarily justify some highly partisan measures. Most governments have followed the example of the Unionists after 1900 and have treated an electoral victory on a specific issue as justification for enacting a whole programme. But, as Ensor points out, 'electoral resentment is apt to accumulate if they do, with such consequences as were seen in 1906 and 1922'.[25]

The victory was very much Chamberlain's. The second-in-command of the smaller section of the Coalition – the Duke was still the leader – appeared in the public eye as by far the most interesting and exciting figure on the government side. It was a very rough election, and it left a lasting bitterness. Liberals freely accused Chamberlain of provoking the war to promote family business interests in the field of armament contracts. Lloyd George raised the matter in December by innuendo in the House, and *Punch* coined a famous phrase: 'The more the Empire expands, the more the Chamberlains contract.'[26] A year later Lloyd George was nearly lynched when he tried to speak in the Birmingham Town Hall. Chamberlain, asked why he had escaped, replied with tight lips: 'What is everybody's business is nobody's business.'

It is unlikely that the government would have won the next general election even if it had been purely Tory. The fact that it was a coalition made its chances even less favourable. In July 1902 Salisbury bowed himself out. He was succeeded by his nephew, Arthur Balfour. Despite much propaganda in the Liberal Unionist press, which was not inspired by Chamberlain, there could have been no other choice, and Chamberlain fully recognised that this was so. Yet, as Denis Judd observes,[27] 'it was impossible to believe that the man who once said that the premiership was the only political position worth having had entirely abandoned all ambition to inhabit 10 Downing Street'. He may well have appreciated the realities of 1902 without necessarily accepting that these were immutable or that he could never reach the top. Certainly he did not choose to efface himself. He had been adamant against fusion before the election of 1895 and he was to continue to be until the end of his active political life. He was determined to preserve what he regarded as his power base.

The solidarity of the Coalition was not outwardly shaken by Salisbury's retirement, but a series of events soon began to weaken it. The most important was Balfour's Education Act. On its merits it must be regarded as one of the great reforming measures of the twentieth

century, and it set up a system which lasted until R. A. Butler's Act of
1944. But from Chamberlain's point of view it was highly damaging.
His support within the Liberal Unionists party came principally from
the Nonconformist voters. But putting the voluntary schools 'on the
rates' the Bill was bound to infuriate them, since such schools were
invariably either Anglican or Roman Catholic. Chamberlain asked
Robert Morant, the formidable civil servant who was the principal
architect of the Bill, why support for the voluntary schools could not
come from central funds. Morant replied, 'Because your War has made
further recourse to State grants impossible'.

   This was not an issue on which Chamberlain could expect solidarity
among the Liberal Unionists. If they had been unanimous, there might
have been a chance of getting the Bill modified, since the Conservatives
on their own commanded rather less than half the House, and the
Liberal Unionists held, though very marginally, the balance of power.[28]
But in any case many Liberal Unionists favoured the Bill, and the Duke
of Devonshire, who was still their leader, strongly supported it. Moreover, as Lord President of the Council he was particularly well placed to
do so, since education came under the general supervision of his office.
A gap thus opened up between two sections of the party, and
Chamberlain, as a conservative defender of the 1870 settlement, found
himself uncomfortably placed on the non-progressive side of it. But he
had to defend the Bill or else resign. He chose to defend it, though he did
so with great reluctance – not because of its merits, to which he was
indifferent, but because of the inevitable loss of Noncomformist votes
and the consequential damage to his Midland base. His reluctance was
enhanced by the fact that the major concession which he had extracted
before the introduction of the Bill was removed when Balfour allowed a
free vote on the question of an option for the local authorities to refuse
to subsidise voluntary schools. The removal of the option made better
educational sense, but it provoked even greater rage among the Radical
Unionists.

   The Bill was carried at the end of 1902. Chamberlain was by now
casting about for a policy to repair the harm done to his section of the
party and to his own prestige. He found it in tariff reform. 'If we had
had no Educational Bill of 1902, we should have had no Tariff Reform
in 1903', wrote Lord George Hamilton, Secretary for India and a strong
free trader.[29] If he meant to suggest that Chamberlain's only motive was
to put himself back on the political map, Hamilton was being less than
fair. Chamberlain undoubtedly believed in reciprocal imperial
preference on its merits, but the vigour and timing of his campaign may
well have been connected with the setbacks which he had received in
1902. Who can say to what extent conscious or subconscious regrets at
missing the succession to Salisbury and at failing to modify the
Education Act led Chamberlain to take his initiative just when he did?

Whatever his motives, his decision altered the course of political history. Tariff Reform split the Conservatives and split the Liberal Unionists. It united the Liberal and Labour Parties and it led to the greatest Tory defeat since 1832.

The history is too familiar to be described here. It is enough to say that Chamberlain's decision to break with the long-established fiscal orthodoxy of free trade resulted in 1903 in a series of dismissals and resignations (including for opposite motives his own and that of the Duke), which gravely weakened Balfour's administration. It was not till 1962 that a similar drastic reconstruction of a Cabinet occurred – although the reasons then were different and the electoral consequences were far less adverse. Balfour tried to steer a middle way between tariff reform and free trade, but his compromise satisfied few people. Joseph Chamberlain's Tariff Reform League by the end of 1904 was challenging the National Union of Conservative and Constitutional Associations, which was the citadel of the faithful, and the free-trader Duke of Devonshire had resigned his leadership of the Liberal Unionists.

It cannot be seriously doubted at this stage that Chamberlain aimed at ousting Balfour and becoming head of a Unionist Party committed to imperial preference. He reckoned on the Liberals winning the next election by about eighty, but not lasting very long and he saw himself leading the Tariff Reformers to victory at the one after. Balfour, however, controlled the date of dissolution and he was for various reasons determined to postpone it for as long as he could. For one thing an election in, say, 1904 or early 1905 would almost certainly have confirmed Chamberlain as the effective ruler of the Unionist party, since the tide of imperial preference was rapidly rising. Tides fall as well as rise. Many of the factors operating in Chamberlain's favour, in particular fear of unemployment, ceased to apply as the months passed. Balfour resigned in December 1905. The ensuing landslide gave the Liberals a victory far greater than Chamberlain's predicted eighty, and it cost Balfour his seat, temporarily.

In 1895 Balfour, twelve years younger than Chamberlain, had said, 'The difference between Joe and me is the difference between youth and age: I am age.'[30] There was much truth in the comment, but age inexorably affects the flesh, even if the spirit is preserved. Two years had passed since the heyday of the Tariff Reform movement. Chamberlain was now seventy and he had never spared himself or stinted himself. All the signs pointed towards his superseding Balfour when suddenly, on 13 July 1906, he was laid low by a paralytic stroke from which he never recovered, though he lingered on, a pitiful wreck, for eight more years. Balfour, chilly, remote, charming and enigmatic as ever, lived till 1930. He was never again to be prime minister though he was to hold high office, and he bequeathed a united party to his successor.

As for the Liberal Unionists, their sense of identity gradually diminished. They continued to be a separate party more from a sense of respect for Joseph Chamberlain than for any other reason, obtaining some 25 seats in 1906 and just over 30 in both the elections of 1910. Ironically this independence may have contributed to one of Joseph's bitterest disappointments in his latter days, the failure of his son Austen to become leader of the Unionists as a whole after Balfour resigned in November 1911. The battle was between him and Walter Long, though in the end both stood down in favour of Bonar Law. Writing to his step-mother about his chances, Austen said: 'Against me, however, there is Long's strong objection ... and the fact that I am both a Liberal Unionist and a Nonconformist.'[31] That the differences of party label were still a reality is shown by the fact that Liberal Unionists had only become eligible for the Carlton Club that year, and the election of Bonar Law was the first occasion when Austen set foot in that Con-servative holy of holies.

Shortly after this, early in 1912, the two organisations were amalgamated. There had long ceased to be any real distinction between them in terms of policy. The divisions which plagued the Unionists from the days of the Education Act onwards were ones that cut across both the Conservative and the Liberal Unionist sections of the alliance. And so the Coalition of 1895, like the Coalition of 1852, led in the end to fusion, and the same was to be true of the Coalition of 1931, though it was not to be true of those of 1915, 1916 and 1940.

No simple lesson emerges from a survey of coalitions before 1900. Clearly they were rare enough to require in each case a special explanation. The first-past-the-post system usually produced a clear verdict for a particular party. Coalitions in Britain were freaks, oddities and deviations from a norm which is single-party government with a clear, if sometimes small, majority.

This norm did not, however, always prevail and there were occasions when the electoral results were not clear or decisive. The Fox–North, the Aberdeen and the Salisbury coalitions were designed to meet basically similar problems – to produce governments which, in an ambiguous parliamentary party situation, could command a majority in the House and carry out a policy. All three coalitions had a feature in common, which may have led to their ultimate failure. Fox, Russell and Chamberlain were ambitious, eloquent and powerful figures who com-manded parties sufficiently large to wreck their coalitions, but were not themselves in the top position. They soon became disruptive forces. The contrast with Baldwin in 1931–5 is obvious.

The three coalitions had another common feature. They only came into being because, in Gladstone's words already quoted about the 1852 Coalition, there was 'a great and palpable emergency of state' in each case to justify this deviation from the normal form – the need to deal with the American war, the problem of income tax, the question of

Home Rule. When these questions became less pressing or, as with George III and Fox, the monarch decided that enough was enough, the coalition quite suddenly began to crumble. Gladstone settled the income tax question in 1853, and, although Aberdeen's Cabinet continued harmoniously for another eighteen months, its real *raison d'être*, apart from meeting a problem of parliamentary arithmetic, had gone. Similarly, the Liberal Unionists had supported Salisbury over Irish Home Rule, 'a great and palpable emergency of state' if ever there was one. But the danger diminished after 1895, and after 1900 seemed even less serious, although in the long run this was to be a delusion. The apparent disappearance of the emergency was bound to weaken the cohesion of the coalition. This is perhaps why coalitions can have a solid basis in war, for the emergency is there till war ends, but why in peace they tend to be uneasy, nervous and insecure after the situation which produced them has been solved or has gone away. There are, however, those who may feel that a nervous and uneasy government is not always to be regarded less favourably than one that is brash and confident. The coalitions of the nineteenth century had a more respectable record than has sometimes been recognised.

# 2  1902-1924

## KENNETH O. MORGAN

'National unity alone can save Britain, can save Europe, can save the world', Lloyd George declared before the somewhat sceptical Liberals gathered at the Manchester Reform Club in December 1919.[1] His theme was that only a coalition, such as Asquith had formed in May 1915 and which he himself had led from December 1916 and on into the post-war years, could provide lasting solutions to the new problems confronting the nation. Only by escaping from the bonds of party warfare could government and parliament pursue fruitful policies for domestic progress and reconstruction, for Ireland and India, for disarmament and international peace. He contrasted the way in which a bipartisan approach had enabled the British parliament to accept the League of Nations covenant, with the bitter partisanship which had destroyed the prospects for the League in the United States congress. But Lloyd George, ever the ingenious advocate of new political alignments and formations, took his thesis still further. He argued that coalition had long been the rule, not the exception, in British politics. He claimed that since the turn of the century, in fact since 1885, Britain had been governed by coalitions, with the brief interlude of the majority Liberal governments of January 1906 to January 1910. There had been no viable alternative in the recent past and there was certainly none at the present time. In peace as in war, 'country before party' offered the rhetoric and the reality that would bring the nation safely through.

Lloyd George's historical analysis, inevitably, was distorted and selective. In the early years of the century, down to the outbreak of world war in 1914, partisanship, not coalition, was the rule of British politics. The bitter party acrimony of the period from 1909 – acrimony to which Lloyd George himself made a considerable contribution – reached levels seldom experienced previously. The end of the war in South Africa in May 1902 had been the signal for a resumption of party warfare in its most belligerent form. There had been those who had speculated that the old conflict between Unionists and Liberals would be transformed by the shock effect of the crisis of empire in South Africa. Perhaps the Liberal Imperialists would make common cause with the Unionists in pursuit of 'national efficiency'. The slate of party contention would be wiped clean, with Rosebery perhaps as strategist-

in-chief of a new government of national unity. On the pro-Boer side,
conversely, some observers claimed to detect signs of a kind of popular
front emerging which would unite anti-war Liberals, the Irish and the
Labour Representation Committee in a new progressive realignment.
Keir Hardie proposed, at various times, Lloyd George, John Burns and
even John Morley as the leader of such a grouping. He wrote in the
*Labour Leader* in 1902 that there was evidence of the dissolution of the
British party system in favour of a series of groups based on
proportional representation on the Swiss model.[2]

But Rosebery and Hardie were both inaccurate prophets. The peace
of Vereeniging in May 1902 released the energies of Unionists and
Liberals alike for party warfare. The issues that divided them at home
remained profound and wide-ranging. The 1902 Education Act found
an Imperialist like Asquith lined up as determinedly as a 'little
Englander' like Lloyd George in opposition to 'Rome on the rates'. The
threat to free trade embodied in Joseph Chamberlain's raising of the
standard of tariff reform in May 1903 made the party battle all the more
vigorous. Indeed, in the years up to the general election of January
1906, the party fluidity of the Boer War period receded into a barely
recognisable past. Tariff reform, it is true, produced some internal
party confusion. A small handful of maverick Liberals, notably Sir
Edward Reed, member for Cardiff, supported tariff reform and joined
the Unionists on imperial grounds. Much more significantly,
Chamberlain's crusade produced immense divisions within the
Unionist ranks, with the defection of Chamberlain himself from the
Cabinet accompanied by that of the free trade ministers, Ritchie and
Devonshire. Balfour, the Prime Minister, had a desperate time in trying
to preserve some façade of party unity during the period 1903–5. But
internal party divisions of this kind were far removed from the idea of
coalition. The government was formally, of course, a coalition of the
Conservative and Liberal Unionist parties; but this carried limited
significance by 1903. The divisions over tariff reform existed within
rather than between the two governmental factions.

One effect of the controversy was Chamberlain's capturing of control
of the Liberal Unionist party machine. Helplessly, Unionist free traders
such as Gorst, Goschen, Devonshire and James of Hereford urged a
possible electoral pact between the Liberals and the 'Unionist free
fooders' at the next election. St Loe Strachey in the *Spectator* was a
powerful advocate of such a policy. But the general intensifying of party
passion from 1903 onwards made the Liberal whips less and less
likely to listen sympathetically. In fact, only in Durham did the local
Liberals give a 'Free Fooder' (Arthur Elliott) a clear run.[3] When the
general election finally came in January 1906, shortly after
Campbell-Bannerman became prime minister, it marked a clear party
confrontation between Liberals and Unionists, in which the middle
ground of the 'Unionist Free Fooders' was swept away from them by

the contending armies. January 1906, with its huge Liberal landslide, was a triumph for party and for the big battalions. Some years later, in 1911–12, the effective absorption of the Liberal Unionist machinery by the Conservatives formally ratified what political pressures had long since made logical and inevitable.

The years of Liberal government that followed down to the January 1910 general election were even more emphatically a period when ideas of coalition disappeared from serious consideration. Initially over the 'Old Liberal' themes of education and temperance, later from 1908 onwards over the 'New Liberal' issues of social reform advanced by Churchill and Lloyd George, the gulf between the major parties became wider than ever. The involvement of the House of Lords, when it rejected Lloyd George's 'people's budget' of 1909, drove partisanship to new heights of bitterness. The January 1910 election, fought on the budget, and that of December 1910, essentially a mandate for the government's Parliament Bill, were both marked by apparently irreconcilable divisions between government and opposition. When the Asquith government finally pushed through its reform of the House of Lords in July–August 1911, the fury of the Unionist opposition knew no bounds. The famous scene when the 'Hughligans' howled Asquith down in the House of Commons symbolised an unparalleled bitterness in political life, whatever the social contacts might be between frontbench politicians as individuals.

Lloyd George himself, the Jacobin mob orator of Limehouse and Newcastle, with his violent onslaughts on the peers, notably inflamed the passions of the hour. Yet it was he, extraordinarily enough, who advanced the only plausible scheme for party collaboration and coalition in the pre-1914 period.[4] This came during the party discussions over a possible compromise over the Lords veto question which followed the accession of George V in May 1910 and lingered on until November. Lloyd George's basic argument was that the needs of a new century made the old party battles irrelevant and even damaging. The House of Lords controversy showed all too clearly how sectional conflict could consume the national energy – in marked contrast to the organised corporate planning he had seen at first hand in Germany in 1908. He argued that Irish home rule, Lords reform, Welsh disestablishment, even free trade could be disposed of on a bipartisan basis as 'non-controversial issues'. Instead, the national effort of a combined Liberal and Unionist government (significantly, Labour was left out) could be devoted to the supreme issues of social reform – national insurance, unemployment, housing, education and temperance – and perhaps to military preparedness as well. His draft coalition programme even hinted at some form of military conscription. It was a clear illustration of Lloyd George's abiding passion for a kind of supreme national synthesis that would soar above petty political partisanship. The 'New Nationalism' of Theodore Roosevelt in the

United States, in which such controversies as trusts and tariffs would be settled by regulatory commissions of non-partisan experts, was a model for the kind of programme Lloyd George had in mind. It kindled some interest among those of a similar cross-bench persuasion –such as the ex-Unionist Churchill on the Liberal side, and F. E. Smith among the Unionists. Lloyd George approached Grey and Balfour as well.

But his schemes, a trailer for 1916, had no hope whatsoever in 1910. Any credible coalition must have some list of agreed political priorities among the party leaders, and preferably among grass-roots enthusiasts as well. In 1910 there was none. Asquith and the Liberals, Austen Chamberlain and the Unionists felt that there was scant common ground between them. Indeed, Smith was the sole Unionist enthusiast. The issues that Lloyd George deemed 'non-controversial' others thought intensely controversial – indeed, they formed the very stuff of politics as commonly understood. Lloyd George's coalition plan, then, got nowhere. Rather it led to a phase of party acrimony even more intense than had occurred before.

The years 1910–14 were again a time when ideas of coalition between the major parties seemed unrealistic and even absurd. After a brief moment of bipartisan accord over the early stages of the 1911 National Insurance bill, party tension mounted. The scandals of the Marconi affair, with their undercurrents of anti-semitism, gave it a more personal flavour. By the summer of 1914, the prospect of an Irish home rule bill being forced through parliament, with perhaps civil war in Ireland itself as the result, made party passions still more inflamed. Unionist leaders from Bonar Law downwards seemed to be encouraging not merely such anachronisms as the use of the royal veto over government legislation, but even resistance to the law of the land in Ulster itself. The Curragh crisis of March 1914 raised Liberal cries (quite inaccurate as it turned out) that the Unionists were putting pressure on military commanders in Ulster to disobey the orders of the lawful civil administration in London. Partisanship, Liberals cried, was taking the Unionists close to treason. Years later, in 1970, Robert Blake could describe Bonar Law's attitude as one of 'atavistic extremism'.[5]

The only glow of the embers of coalition in this period, perhaps, may be seen in the relations of the Liberal government and their allies on whose votes they had depended for a majority in the House since 1910 – the Irish Nationalists and the Labour Party. But neither relationship could really be termed a coalition in any precise sense. The Irish Nationalists, bound to the Liberal party since 1886 would, of course, support the government only on the assumption that the Liberals would make Irish home rule their major political priority. The Irish were basically a one-issue party: since 1910 their pressure had forced Asquith to bring forward a much-delayed third Home Rule Bill. But the Irish always maintained a position of rigid independence towards the

Westminster government; their eighty-odd members sat, symbolically, in permanent opposition. Instructions to Irish electors in England, Wales and Scotland to vote Liberal did not imply any direct involvement of the Irish Nationalist party in the processes of government. Indeed, such involvement would have spelt the immediate doom of Redmond, Dillon and their followers.

Similarly, the Labour Party, which had maintained a secret electoral entente with the Liberal whips since 1903, also fiercely treasured its independence, however much zealots in the ILP might complain that the Liberal and Labour parties were becoming indistinguishable. The government and Labour's new leader, Ramsay MacDonald, consorted on tactics in 1911. In return for the passage of the payment of M.P.s, MacDonald promised that Labour would support the government's National Insurance bill. However, he had the greatest of difficulty in delivering Labour's votes as promised – Snowden, Lansbury, Jowett and eventually Keir Hardie, among others, came out in opposition to the 'poll-tax' embodied in Lloyd George's contributory scheme. Labour's independence from the Liberals was underlined anew. Nor would the Liberals try to support Labour's 'right to work' bill on unemployment.

On only one occasion was there a direct overture from the Liberals to Labour on behalf of a coalition. In March 1914, around the time of the Curragh crisis, at first through the mediation of the back-bench Liberal, Josiah Wedgwood, and later through Lloyd George, an offer of coalition was made to MacDonald. In return for a closer relationship between Labour and the Liberals, he would be given a seat in Asquith's cabinet.[6] Perhaps a newly-defined progressive alliance would go the country later in the year on a 'who governs Britain?' platform, binding reformers of all shades together against the food taxers, Ulster covenanters, peers, militarists and clericalists within the Unionist ranks. MacDonald may well have been temporarily attracted by the idea – so might Henderson, perhaps. But there was never any chance of the Labour Party's agreeing. The executive council of the ILP was only one of the organs within the 'Labour alliance' which totally rejected any sacrifice of their movement's cherished independence. It would betray everything Labour had fought for since Hardie challenged the Liberal machine in Mid-Lanark back in 1888. Any such agreement by MacDonald would have meant his downfall as party leader just as surely as did his later acquiescence in coalition in the traumatic days of August 1931. The government's allies, then, remained wholly distinct entities, quite outside the process of governing. There was nothing remotely resembling the intimate relationship foreshadowed in the 'consultative committee' arrangements worked out by James Callaghan and David Steel over half a century later, in March 1977, when a minority Labour government depended on a tiny Liberal group for its continuance in office.

The summer of 1914 came with government ministers and opposition leaders toiling through the muddy by-ways of Tyrone and Fermanagh in a hopeless search for a compromise over the status of Ulster, and with partisanship reaching a new crescendo. Indeed, just as the crises of the time widened the gulf between the parties, so they induced a new coherence and discipline within the parties. Revolt against the whips was seldom less fashionable. In particular, the Liberals, ever prone to sectional or 'faddist' divisions internally since the days of the 1891 Newcastle Programme, had never seemed more united, never more convinced of the holy righteousness of their cause nor more certain of the base iniquity of their opponents. With the added pressures of 'industrial action' in the labour world, the excesses of the women suffragettes and episcopal lamentations over Welsh endowments all adding to the frenzy of the time, it is not surprising that people overseas saw Britain as a land caught up in a kind of anarchy, with extreme political militancy as its major cause.

The situation, of course, was transformed by the outbreak of world war on 4 August 1914. Within a matter of weeks, the partisanship of that interminably long, hot summer melted away. Liberals, Unionists and Labour came together in a mood of national reconciliation to meet the new crisis. Even the Irish Nationalists declared their loyalty to Crown and country, and volunteers came forward in vast numbers in Ireland to enlist in the armed forces. The Labour Party national executive endorsed the decision to go to war. Within four days of Britain's declaring war on Germany, Asquith was writing to Bonar Law to urge that there be a suspension of party controversy. By 28 August this had been taken further. Illingworth, Edmund Talbot and Henderson, the whips of the Liberal, Unionist and Labour parties respectively, signed an agreement which laid down that there should not be a contested election in the event of any parliamentary vacancy occurring up to 1 January 1915.[7] This was resumed at roughly three-monthly intervals until 31 December 1916. A significant alteration was made to the wording in March 1915 to cover the resignation of a member: the point here was to ensure that M.P.s had 'some good cause' before they could be allowed to accept the Chiltern Hundreds. In such cases, the three party whips would have to confer beforehand. This party truce worked with remarkable smoothness. Such constituency difficulties as occurred – for instance, in Swansea District in November 1914 when the Local Liberal Association rejected C. F. G. Masterman as candidate[8] – arose from internal disagreements within local party caucuses, not from disputes between the national parties. Asquith continued as Liberal prime minister from August 1914 with apparently assured all-party support in the House and the country. The suspension of the general election provisions of the Parliament Act underlined his security.

However, a party truce fell far short of a coalition. It was a very uneasy relationship that existed between the two front benches in the autumn of 1914 and the spring of 1915. Immense bitterness had been caused on 14 September by Asquith's insistence on going ahead with the passage of the Irish home rule and Welsh disestablishment bills, despite the vehement hostility of the Unionists to both measures. Bonar Law led his followers out of the House in protest at what he saw as a betrayal of the pledges about avoiding party contention. It was true that both the Irish and the Welsh bills were suspended in their operation until the end of the war. But Unionists pointed out that, in the case of the Welsh bill at least, the Church commissioners would proceed with their work of assessing the value of the Church's endowments, and that disendowment (which many Unionists regarded as a plundering of Church property) would continue, war or no war. By the spring of 1915, Unionists were generally unhappy at the consequences of the party truce. While they undertook to suspend their own machinery and propaganda work in the country, the government went on with its programme of controversial domestic legislation. 'The political truce is wearing very thin', wrote Walter Runciman in February 1915.[9] Unionist back-benchers in particular were discontented with the political limbo into which they had been thrust in August 1914. The formation of the Unionist Business Committee, under the chairmanship of W. A. S. Hewins, while not overtly a challenge to Bonar Law's leadership of the party, was a focus for back-bench protests on tariff and trade policies. Lloyd George's extraordinary schemes in March – April 1915 for a state purchase of the liquor trade heightened Unionist alarm. The Unionist Business Committee led the clamour against these wanton assaults on their traditional allies, the brewers. They even consorted with the Irish Nationalists in rejecting the Chancellor's proposed increased duties on the drink trade.[10] Clearly the wartime truce was wearing thin indeed.

In May 1915, the pressure exploded. Asquith emerged as the head of a national coalition of Liberals, Unionists and Labour. It was a fundamental break with years of partisanship. But the party affiliations of the recent past could not be disposed of so easily. On the contrary, the Asquith coalition of May 1915 to December 1916 was the most precarious of shotgun marriages. It had arisen in very curious circumstances. It was the product of desperate efforts to maintain their credibility by the two party leaders, Bonar Law and Asquith. Law, the target for much back-bench sniping for several months, found two new crises in May likely to undermine his authority. The supposed 'scandal' of the shell shortage, and the resignation of Fisher from the Admiralty after a violent quarrel with Churchill, together provoked an explosion of discontent from the Unionist rank and file. To forestall it, Law had no alternative but to propose a coalition to Asquith. For his part, the Liberal premier was agreeable – but it must be coalition on the Liberals' party terms. While some Liberals were sacrificed (notably Haldane, the victim of an extraordinary anti-German phobia), the new coalition clearly displayed the continued dominance of the Liberal Party. The main offices were occupied by Liberals: Grey stayed at the Foreign Office, McKenna went to the Treasury, Simon to the Home Office. Most crucial of all, Lloyd George, about whose loyalty to his leader there had been some murmurings in the Liberal press, agreed to go to the newly-formed Ministry of Munitions. It was a move that both ensured the success of Asquith's manoeuvres, as an ecstatic premier acknowledged in writing to Lloyd George,[11] and also made the ministry much more dependent on the Welshman. The Unionists fared relatively poorly in the allocation of government posts, Bonar Law himself receiving merely the Colonial Office. Labour's token Cabinet minister was Arthur Henderson, who went to the Education Board. It was the most precarious and unpredictable of governments, the product of intrigue and manoeuvre, with no agreed line of policy for the future. Its essential justification was that it existed to keep the 'pacifists' of the ILP and the Union of Democratic Control firmly at bay, and to fight the war to the bitter end.

The history of Asquith's coalition until its collapse in December 1916 was a poor advertisement for bipartisanship, for all the unifying pressures of world war. On the surface, it is true, the party truce survived. Down to the end of November 1916, there were six vacancies in seats held by the Unionists, and five in Liberal seats. In every case, the party whips immediately agreed not to contest the election and to give the party in possession a clear run.[12] At Westminster, the contentious legislation of pre-war years was quietly set aside. At the same time, it is clear that the mood of coalition was very superficial. The issue that above all others subjected it to strain was that of military conscription. It is true that the divisions that rent the Cabinet on this question between October 1915 and April 1916 did not follow strict party lines. The most ardent 'compulsionist' was Lloyd George himself, now ranged firmly in alliance with such Unionists as Law and Curzon. Behind him, the Liberal War Committee of forty backbenchers pressed for a more vigorous and committed approach to the running of the war. But it is clear that it was largely upon the Liberals that the strains of conscription fell. One Liberal minister, Sir John Simon, the Home Secretary, resigned from the government on the question in January 1916; others, notably McKenna, Runciman and Harcourt, together with Asquith himself, faced torments of conscience. The government, in the view of many Liberals, might be all-party in composition, but it was pursuing Tory policies, and was jettisoning traditional Liberal principles in relation to freedom of conscience and individual liberties. The Allied economic conference at Paris in June 1916 seemed to undermine the fabric of free trade as well, by imposing protective tariffs.

Liberal discontent with the government increased when Lloyd George went to the War Office in succession to Kitchener in July 1916 – a symbol of the growing gulf between him and almost all his Liberal Cabinet colleagues. On the Unionist side, the Unionist War Committee, formed in January 1916 under the leadership of Sir Frederick Banbury and Ronald McNeill, continued to ventilate party unease over conscription, an attempted Irish settlement and trade policy. By the autumn of 1916, the coalition, with its policies apparently yielding only disaster in every theatre of the war, was under fire from many directions. There were pressures from Northcliffe and other press lords for a new approach to the supreme command, with a restructuring of the cabinet. Milner and his imperialist associates of the *Round Table* group were pressing for a new kind of all-party or supra-party government. Lloyd George was profoundly discontented. After the failure to aid Romania in the autumn of 1916, he was on the verge of resignation. Asquith's leadership seemed unconvincing, his government an uneasy compromise between party and coalition rule. By December 1916 Britain was deep in political crisis.

The outcome was that one coalition gave way to another, a coalition much more narrowly based than its predecessor but that was to prove much more effective. The roots of this lay in the political crisis of 1–7 December 1916. Asquith's coalition eighteen months earlier had been conceived within an orthodox party framework; Lloyd George's, formed when the war crisis was far more desperate, was defined in terms of policies and personalities. In a way that was unthinkable to the architects of the coalition in May 1915, the style of the new prime minister in December 1916 was crucial to the new government. His coalition, it is true, also originated in terms of party considerations. Bonar Law, shaken by a back-bench revolt led by Carson over the sale of enemy assets in West Africa, entered into discussion with Carson and Lloyd George in late November over a remodelling of the government. Their scheme for a three-man War Committee presupposed that Asquith would remain prime minister, with an ultimate right of veto over policy. When Asquith unexpectedly threw the scheme over on the morning of 4 December 1916, however, the party pressures all led to the one conclusion. While Unionists, even the dithering 'three C's' (Chamberlain, Cecil and Curzon), rapidly joined the cause of national unity and by 6 December were prepared even to suppress their long-held distaste for Lloyd George, Liberals faced appalling divisions within their ranks.

The result was that Lloyd George took office on 7 December at the head of a genuine all-party coalition, but one obviously dominated by the Unionists. In the five-man War Cabinet, he was the sole Liberal, as against three Unionists (Law, Curzon and Milner) and one Labour man (Henderson). Further, elsewhere in the government, there was only one

Liberal minister of any stature, Lloyd George's loyal supporter
Dr Christopher Addison, who went to the Ministry of Munitions.
Nearly all the leading figures in the Liberal Party were either
ambivalent or directly opposed to the new government. The coalition
faced, from the start, party enmity of a kind quite unknown to
Churchill in 1940–5. On the other hand, Lloyd George had been told
that he commanded the probable support of at least 120 Liberal M.P.s,
almost half the parliamentary Liberal Party. Equally crucial, the
Labour Party's national executive, by a majority of one, decided to
back the new government, and Henderson served in the War Cabinet,
with Clynes, Hodge and Roberts as other Labour ministers lower down
the government. This was altogether a strange new administration that
arose from the ashes of Asquith's regime. It was a government of
fractions of parties, with only the Unionists unequivocally giving it
support; its head served as an individual and in no sense as a party
leader. Its essential elements of stability arose from the temporary
authority of the new prime minister on personal grounds, and from the
sense of overwhelming national crisis at a supreme moment of the war.

Few at first expected the new Lloyd George coalition to survive for any
length of time. The new prime minister, as has been seen, depended
entirely at first on the loyalty and goodwill of his old enemies, the
Unionists. Yet this new government was to prove one of the very few
truly successful coalitions in our history. Its agenda consisted simply of
winning the war. In the fullness of time, this was to be emphatically
achieved. The mechanics of party unity were sustained as they had been
under Asquith down to the end of 1917; they continued *de facto*
thereafter. Things were more difficult now since there was a Lloyd
George Liberal whip, Captain Freddie Guest (who succeeded Neil
Primrose), in implicit rivalry with the official Liberal whip, J. W.
Gulland. This made negotiations about by-elections in effect quadri-
partite, and much more delicate than before. Even so, the party truce
was maintained without great difficulty. Local party machines were
successfully steam-rollered by their head offices, as when Albert Stanley,
the new President of the Board of Trade, was spatchcocked into
Ashton-under-Lyne in succession to the ennobled Max Aitken. In the
same month, December 1916, the veteran Conservative M.P. for
Sheffield, Hallam, was given a peerage and the local Conservatives
were persuaded to hand on the seat to the Liberal H. A. L. Fisher (who
was Vice-Chancellor of Sheffield University and who had just become
President of the Board of Education) on the understanding that the
arrangement was only for the duration of the Parliament. There were, it
is true, several contested by-elections in 1917 and 1918, but these were
invariably the result of the intervention of independent candidates who
sought a more aggressive prosecution of the war. Some of them were

backed by the egregious Pemberton Billing (himself successful in
defeating a Unionist in the East Hertfordshire by-election in March
1916). One was successful – Ben Tillett, who won North Salford in
November 1917 with a programme that combined support for the war
effort with a series of labour demands. 'Anti-profiteering' was one of
Tillett's most popular lines of attack. These by-elections provided a
safety-valve for Liberal or Labour voters to display their vague
discontent with what was (on paper) a largely right-wing coalition. But
they did not seriously disturb relations between the coalitionist party
machines or upset the plausible claim of the government to be national
in character.

As time went on, Lloyd George's administration became more clearly
all-party and broad-based in form. In July 1917, he strengthened its
Liberal representation significantly by bringing in Winston Churchill
and Edwin Montagu, two impressive figures, to Munitions and the
India Office respectively. Apart from powerfully reinforcing the
government's debating strength in the Commons, this 'coup de main'
(as Lord Derby called it)[13] enabled Lloyd George to emphasise his claim
that the administration was Liberal as well as Unionist in tone. The
move of Dr Addison from Munitions to a new Ministry of
Reconstruction (where he was encouraged by the prime minister to
produce a series of imaginative papers on post-war social reconstruction on the lines of the 'new Liberalism' before 1914) underlined the part played in the coalition's policies by the premier's radical
allies. In any case, there seemed to be less and less evidence of party
conflict within the government as time went on. The great debates
within the cabinet over strategy, notably those in June 1917 over the
wisdom of a new offensive in Flanders by Haig, had no obvious party
basis.[14] Lloyd George's defeat in Cabinet, and the resulting débâcle at
Passchendaele with horrendous loss of life, was in no sense a victory for
the Unionists. Indeed, Bonar Law, whose relationship with Lloyd
George was becoming increasingly intimate, was himself severely
shaken by what he took to be Haig's lack of judgement (and perhaps
lack of candour) in pressing on with the Flanders offensive. The great
debates that raged that winter and the following spring over whether to
press on with further offensives on the Western Front, or to concentrate
on peripheral strategy in the Mediterranean and Italy until the
Americans sent reinforcements to France, were debates between
advocates of policies, not between partisans.

In fact, the government was more and more assuming a non-partisan,
indeed non-political, character. In lesser departments, uncommitted
businessmen such as Sir Eric Geddes, Sir Joseph Maclay, Lord
Devonport and Lord Rhondda were being brought in to run departments on businesslike lines within an increasingly corporate state.
Some of them, such as Maclay, never actually confronted parliament at

all. At the centre of government, a mighty new apparatus of government, symbolised by the Cabinet secretariat under Hankey and by the prime minister's secretariat or 'Garden Suburb', emphasised how different Lloyd George's government was from the party-based administrations of pre-1915. The leading figures of the Garden Suburb were W. G. S. Adams, an Oxford professor; Waldorf Astor, the millionaire proprietor of the *Observer*; Joseph Davies, a commercial statistician; and Philip Kerr, a journalist of visionary or even mystical outlook – all stood quite outside the party scene. They encouraged the prime minister, in Kerr's words, to soar above the 'ding-dong' of party controversy.[15] The influence of the Garden Suburb was often exaggerated at the time and has often been since; but its very existence showed that a new leviathan of central administration, bureaucratic and corporatist, had come into being. Equally in the War Cabinet, as has been noted, party considerations seldom disturbed the prime minister's assessment of events. By the spring of 1918, the dominant personality in the Cabinet was Milner, nominally a Unionist, really a kind of Bismarckian state socialist, a man almost arrogant in his detachment from the party scene. His creed of 'social imperialism', while similar to that of the prime minister, was far removed from pre-war shibboleths. If Milner's presence in the Cabinet and its 'X Committee' suggested the truly supra-party aspect of Lloyd George's government, that of General Smuts did so even more decisively. Brought into the Cabinet in 1917 to indicate the imperial character of the war effort, Smuts, a South African, with necessarily no connection at all with the British party or parliamentary scene, showed how traditional party politics were now in suspense, perhaps never to return.

Within the ranks of the administration, then, Lloyd George had less and less trouble as time went on in keeping up a genuinely coalitionist appearance. Nor did the presence of an opposition in the House of Commons, with Asquith as its effective leader, seriously disturb the coalition either. After December 1916, as before, politics continued to be run from the front benches. An unspoken pact existed between the two sides not to turn the government out. Asquith, full of bitterness after the unhappy circumstances of his downfall, was certainly willing to wound, if reluctant to strike. In the furore over the departure of General Robertson as Chief of the Imperial General Staff in February 1918, Asquith showed some inclination to support the military against the civilian commanders, until Robertson's lack of support, even from Haig, ended the crisis. Asquith and the non-governmental Liberals also grumbled intermittently about the government's handling of the Irish question – the failure of the all-Irish convention, the threatened imposition of conscription, hardline Dublin Castle rule, and the resultant dangerous upsurge of Sinn Fein. Most serious of all, Asquith moved what was almost a motion of no confidence in the government on 9 May 1918 after General Maurice's allegations in the newspapers that Lloyd George had starved the army on the Western Front of reinforcements, and that the number of combatant troops in France was actually less in January 1918 than a year earlier. Even here, though, Asquith was half-hearted. Lloyd George won an easy rhetorical triumph on the basis of a very dubious case; only 98 Liberal supporters of Asquith, plus a few others, voted against him in the lobbies. It was the most critical parliamentary challenge that he faced during the years of wartime coalition – and it proved the rule. In practice, Asquith had no realistic policy to propound. The Unionists all supported the government, while the only alternative would have been a return of Asquith himself, a discredited and somewhat pathetic figure, to Downing Street. In practice, then, by maintaining (or being forced to maintain) the unspoken alliance between government and opposition, Asquith was acting as a prop for the coalition himself. With parliament unable to turn the government out, and party politics in the country largely suspended, there was little that disenchanted Liberals could do.

Labour was, perhaps, a more serious threat. Arthur Henderson left the government in August 1917 after a celebrated row with Lloyd George over attendance at an international socialist conference at Stockholm. Labour then built up its party machinery throughout the country and was clearly poised to challenge the government at the next election. Still, Labour's challenge to the coalition mood was a muted one. The party continued to be represented in the government, and showed no inclination to ally with the Asquithian Liberals. Barnes took Henderson's place in the War Cabinet. Lloyd George could at least plausibly claim that 'patriotic' Labour supported him, as did the official leadership of the Labour Party and the TUC, whatever the anti-war fever stirring within the ranks of the ILP and in such industrial movements as the shop stewards of Clydeside. There was opposition to the coalition in mid-1918, certainly. But it was extra-parliamentary and almost extra-political – rank-and-file movements amongst the Welsh miners, the engineers and shipyard workers; pacifist bodies such as the No Conscription Fellowship; outright opponents such as Sinn Fein and the IRA in southern Ireland. It did not seriously undermine the government's claim to be a national one or to embody all the significant strains in the political culture of Britain, outside Ireland.

Lloyd George's coalition, then, seemed increasingly impregnable in wartime – but it was war alone that had brought it about. Some day, perhaps when the impact of American military help was felt on the Western Front, peace would return, and what would become of coalition then? Gradually in the course of 1918 Lloyd George and his coalitionist supporters took steps to ensure that the government would survive into the post-war era. Obviously the outstanding problem that the prime minister faced was that he had no party, not even the merest vestiges of one, since the official Liberal machinery and constituency organisation were firmly in Asquithian hands. Addison met with Waldorf Astor and Victor Fisher of the British Workers' League (a most curious trio) in December 1917 to try to suggest how the prime minister could invent a political machine. Lord Riddell of the *News of the World* and Sir William Sutherland, the premier's press and patronage secretary, also offered eccentric advice. But it was not until May 1918, just after the Maurice debate, that steps were taken to set up a 'Coalition Liberal' organisation, under Guest as chief whip.[16] This was the crucial step towards forming a viable peacetime coalition, rather than one in which Lloyd George was a lonely hostage to the Unionist majority. Now he could bargain with the Unionist whips on something like equal terms. The electoral agreement made in July 1918 was the basis of it all – the notorious 'coupon' or official letter of government endorsement which would be sent to all candidates, Unionist, Liberal or Labour, who were deemed (after a somewhat haphazard process of selection) to be supporters of the government. Furthermore, in the course of negotiations, while it was acknowledged that the Unionists would provide the majority of the 'couponed' candidates, the Coalition Liberals did remarkably well in the allocation of seats. In the end, 150 constituencies, a nice round number that was said to have been suggested by the prime minister himself,[17] was the respectable tally that the Liberals could claim. A hundred of them, wrote Guest, were 'our Old Guard'.[18] A smaller number was allocated to the National Democratic Party, a pro-government 'patriotic Labour' splinter group. The 'coupon' arrangement was originally framed with a wartime election in mind. It was assumed that the war would drag on until mid-1920 or so. However, with the sudden German collapse after August, it became clear that the 'coupon' would form the basis of a contest between the coalition and its mixed bag of opponents as soon as an armistice was declared.

In October, Lloyd George and Bonar Law hammered out a policy as well, a manifesto which provided reasonable compromises over Ireland, India, free trade and other contentious matters, but which contained a clear Liberal emphasis, especially in its ringing endorsement of a sweeping programme of social reform and reconstruction. The Liberal 'Policy for Government Committee' which Addison had chaired the previous July, had clearly borne fruit.[19] When peace came on 11 November it soon became clear that the coalition which would go to the country would be an incomplete one. Labour, predictably, announced its immediate withdrawal from the government. Bernard Shaw achieved his great rhetorical triumph here – 'Go back to Lloyd George and say "Nothing Doing"'. The followers of Asquith were ostracised, all the more so as their leader had refused a somewhat half-hearted offer of the Lord Chancellorship from Lloyd George. Still, the party basis of the government was wide enough to lend it a truly national aspect. Almost all the Unionist candidates in the field were 'couponed' supporters of the coalition. The allocation of 150 Coalition Liberals was satisfactory enough on Lloyd George's side. At a meeting of Liberal M.P.s on 12 November a motion in favour of endorsing the coalition, moved by H. A. L. Fisher and endorsed by such as Churchill, Addison, Montagu and Mond, was overwhelmingly accepted. Even the Labour support for the government was not negligible. Quite apart from the two dozen NDP candidates, such official Labour men as J. H. Thomas and Vernon Hartshorn made it clear that they warmly endorsed the government's wartime policies and sought a punitive settlement for the defeated 'Huns'. The 'coupon' arrangements were not accepted in the constituencies without some problems. Local Unionist and Liberal party workers complained that their own safe seats had been casually handed over by the whips to the other side. Unionists were especially indignant at the unduly generous terms granted to the Coalition Liberals: Lord Salisbury complained bitterly that a Unionist seat in Wandsworth had been given on a plate to Freddie Guest himself.[20] In a few cases, notably in Swansea West, where Sir Alfred Mond aroused much local animosity, partly on anti-semitic grounds,[21] local Unionists actually rejected the 'coupon' arrangements and put up independent candidates against the coalition nominees.

Overall, though, it is striking how little difficulty the transition from a wartime to a peacetime coalition caused. Of course, the hysteria and jingoism of a 'khaki election' helped mightily in this respect. In constituency after constituency, Liberal 'pacifists' and Labour 'Bolsheviks' were routed. The Asquithians returned barely twenty members; their leader was amongst the fallen, at East Fife. Labour, which polled a significantly high vote, managed to return only 57 members; MacDonald, Snowden, Henderson and others marked out as critics of the war were annihilated. The election left many questions unanswered. The Coalition Unionists and Coalition Liberals were two quite distinct parties and future relationships between them were obscure. Seymour Cocks of the ILP thought that Coalition Liberals not actually in the government might take over the Opposition benches 'and, in a sort of alliance with the pro-war Labourites, constitute themselves a kind of very friendly opposition in order to damp down all criticism'. Horatio Bottomley was thought to be another claimant for the post of leader of the Opposition.[22] But the authority of the new coalition and its national appeal were not in doubt. Politician after politician declared, with all sincerity, that the issues of pre-war were out-of-date, that the new problems of peace and reconstruction demanded national rather than party solutions. Bonar Law, writing to Balfour before the election, had viewed with equanimity the prospect of Lloyd George leading the Unionists into the post-war world. 'I am perfectly

certain that our party on the old lines will never have any future again in
this country.' The old controversies over land or liquor belonged to an
irrelevant past. 'Unless there is some combination of parties such as
would be secured by L. G. and his friends working with us', the result
would be that social and economic issues would be pressed only by the
Liberal and Labour parties, with the Unionists left with the sterile role of
permanent opposition.[23] The only answer was a bipartisan government
which would steer between the shoals of the diehards and the
revolutionaries. After the election results were declared, with their
massive landslide majority for the coalition, Bonar Law's commitment
to bipartisanship was reinforced. Quite apart from the magnitude of the
problems confronting Britain and the world, there was the towering
personal ascendancy of the prime minister. No one had ever attained
such overwhelming authority; he could be 'prime minister for life' if he
liked.[24] If the Unionists did not hang together alongside the quasi-
presidential figure of Lloyd George and his Liberal camp followers,
they would assuredly hang separately.

The new coalition of Lloyd George lasted from December 1918 to
October 1922. It was the longest-lasting peacetime coalition in modern
British history with the technical exception of 1931–9 when a single
party was in fact dominant. From the start, it showed a genuine trans-
party character. The peacetime cabinet which was restored in October
1919 contained eleven Unionists, eight Liberals and one Labour man,
with a similar admixture at the junior ministerial levels. The party
balance was a genuine reflection of the course of the government.
Accusations that Liberal principles and policies were being steam-
rollered by the Unionist majority had little substance. The party
balance certainly altered as time went on – and as Lloyd George's initial
dazzling authority began to decline. In February 1920, the Labour
element in the government was largely removed by the almost simul-
taneous resignations of Barnes and G. H. Roberts. Thereafter, any
claim of the coalition to represent Labour was plainly fraudulent, as the
resurgence of Labour in by-elections from Spen Valley (January 1920)
onwards testified. Coalition Liberal representation in the government
was also seriously eroded. In July 1921, after a savage public brawl with
Lloyd George, Addison, for long a vehement supporter of the coalition
and its most energetic social reformer, was forced out of the government. His departure symbolised the end of the government's effective
commitment to social reform, and to new house-building and slum
clearance in particular. Another outspoken casualty in March 1922 was
Edwin Montagu, another radical Liberal, who departed in violent
protest about the government's pro-Greek policy in the Near East and
the way in which Lloyd George's anti-Turk manoeuvres were inflaming
Moslem opinion in India. The Liberal element in the government was

severely weakened as a result. Still, important ministers remained, such
as Fisher, Mond, Macnamara, Short and, of course, Churchill (still
nominally a Liberal); and throughout early 1922 there were rumours
that the newly-christened National Liberal Party would demand a new
bargain with the Unionists to replace that of 1918. McCurdy, the
Coalition Liberal chief whip, kept up a stream of confident (if
misconceived) memoranda to the prime minister to this effect.[25] Right
down to the end, the coalition retained a genuinely bipartisan aspect,
with its predominantly Unionist ministers still in major respects
dependent on the Liberal prime minister. Neither in its politics nor in its
composition did the coalition of 1919–22 suppress its Liberalism; the
Coalition Liberals were far more vigorous and independent than either
the National Liberal or the National Labour groups were to be in the
government of 1931–5. At one important level, the Home Affairs
Committee of the Cabinet, which under H. A. L. Fisher, dominated
domestic legislation in 1919–21, had a clear Liberal preponderance in
it,[26] and was accused by one critic of almost turning into 'a bill factory'.
By contrast, the other major Cabinet committee, the Finance
Committee, was chaired by the prime minister, with Austen Chamberlain its dominant figure. In general, it is the absence of partisan feeling
within the government that is impressive. Sir Robert Horne's pro-
nouncement to the Cambridge University Conservatives in November
1921 (given as the verdict of 'a Disraelian Tory') that he had never
known a major issue to be discussed in Cabinet on party lines had the
clear ring of truth,[27] and a modern historian would confirm it.

Of course, party divisions sometimes did intrude. The Coalition
Liberals did show signs of unrest over some major issues. Free trade
was a frequent source of friction. Anti-dumping legislation, provisions
to protect home manufacturers against 'collapsed exchanges' such as
the German mark, the imperial preference contained in Chamberlain's
budget of 1919 – all seemed to be subtly undermining the free trade
heritage of Cobden and Gladstone. Several Coalition Liberal ministers
protested against the 1921 Safeguarding of Industry Bill in Cabinet.
When Wedgwood Benn introduced a motion to repeal it in February
1922, the Coalition Liberal M.P.s voted 19 – 18 in favour of it, while a
further 87 abstained or were absent. These last included four Cabinet
ministers (Shortt, Munro, McCurdy and Churchill). The policy of
'retaliation' in Ireland through the 'Black and Tans' and the 'Auxis' also
gave rise to protests by Liberal ministers. Fisher, Addison and
Montagu were foremost among those who called for more conciliatory
and less coercive policies.[28] On the other hand, the Irish Office was in
Liberal hands – MacPherson being followed by Hamar Greenwood –
and the 1920 Government of Ireland Act could be defended on
traditional Liberal grounds as a 'home rule' solution. On the whole, the
Liberal ministers and their back-bench supporters were uneasy less at

the course of government policy, which was recognised as being far
from reactionary on most issues, than at the gulf which divided them
from their Asquithian brethren. After the uproar at the National
Liberal Federation meeting at Leamington Spa in May 1920, when the
Coalition Liberal ministers, with Addison, Hewart and Kellaway at
their head, were proscribed by the Asquithian majority and in effect
drummed out of the party, the 'Coaly Libs' were an unhappy crew. The
severance from the Independent Liberals was politically logical, but
politics is as much emotion as logic, and the schism brought pain and
heart-searching. But there was no other route the Coalitionists could
choose other than continuing to support the government. In practice,
then, even during the traumatic events of the 'Geddes Axe' which laid
low most of the social programmes to which the Liberals were
committed, the loyalty of the Coalition Liberals to the government for
which they supplied a leader was assured.

The loyalty of the dominant Unionists was harder to guarantee, and
obviously much more crucial to the future of the government. Unionists
in the country and in parliament witnessed with growing alarm the free-
spending programmes of Liberal ministers. Addison, as Minister of
Health and Housing, was the particular target for their wrath. His
expensive subsidies to private builders, via the local authorities, to try to
stimulate the housing programme, were grist to the mill of 'anti-waste'
zealots. Fisher, as Minister of Education, and Mond, First Commissioner of Works, were not far behind in 'anti-waste' demon-
ology. Here and elsewhere, it seemed to Unionists that, far from
their swallowing up Lloyd George, it was the prime minister who was
playing the whale to their Jonah. On India, Montagu's liberal policies,
especially the dismissal of General Dyer after the atrocities at Amritsar
were another source of violent discontent. In the autumn of 1921,
Unionist alarm with the policies of the coalition mounted. The eventual
outcome of the Irish troubles was the Free State treaty of December
1921, negotiated with Sinn Fein, which accorded an extreme degree of
independence to the twenty-six Catholic counties of southern Ireland,
and left Ulster in the lurch and unprotected against IRA reprisals. A
wave of IRA atrocites in early 1922, culminating in the murder of Field-
Marshal Sir Henry Wilson outside his home in Eaton Square, London,
added to their fears.

Again, in foreign policy, Unionists watched Lloyd George's
manoeuvres with anxiety. In particular, the approach to the Genoa
conference due to be convened in April 1922 seemed most disturbing.
The proposal to grant *de jure* recognition to Soviet Russia, and to try
to bring the Bolsheviks and also the defeated Germans (whose
reparations Lloyd George was anxious to scale down) into the
European diplomatic and financial system all roused Unionist fears.
Wickham Steed in *The Times*, with some most irresponsible reporting,
fanned the flames, while Churchill, with his obsessive anti-Bolshevism,

joined the Unionist critics. In March 1922, Lloyd George was in effect voted down by a majority of his own Cabinet over the formal recognition of the Soviet Union. He had to propose instead a humiliating compromise with only *chargés d'affaires* in Moscow and London instead of official ambassadors being accepted by Britain.[29] Here again, the Prime Minister seemed to many Unionists to be lurching too far in a Liberal direction and carrying them with him. The Prime Minister was also thought to be indulging in a 'swing to the left' on the home front in the winter of 1921–22, with his new emphasis on policies to remedy unemployment and to revive trade. It appeared that he might try to challenge Labour head-on and claim that it was the government which had the truly radical social and industrial policy. It had preserved industrial peace and frustrated the Triple Alliance, but by liberal and humane rather than reactionary measures. Meanwhile 'waste' went on, and such cherished Tory ambitions as the reform of the House of Lords to make it a more effective chamber were left unfulfilled.

Even so, until the government's policies began to go seriously awry after the failure of the Genoa conference in April–May 1922, Unionist discontent with the course of policy was generally contained. The Unionist protests usually manifested themselves in by-elections, where a series of candidates were nominated under Unionist credentials, only to denounce the government for waste and opportunism. The coalition, complained Lord Salisbury, was a synonym for extravagance and dishonesty,[30] and most grass-roots Unionists probably agreed with him. But these by-election pinpricks were safely withstood by the 'cheerful pachyderm', as *Punch* depicted Lloyd George. The by-election heroes entered the Commons and their protests subsided: Esmond Harmsworth, for instance, who was elected for the Isle of Thanet on an anti-Waste ticket, had served on the prime minister's personal staff. The National Union of Conservative Associations, which often rang with protests against Unionist adherence to the coalition, could nevertheless pass declarations of loyalty to the coalition time and again, down to the end of 1921. Above all, the 'diehard' rebels in the constituencies had no credible leader – none more charismatic than Sir Henry Page Croft or Sir Frederick Banbury. All the leading Unionists – Law, Austen Chamberlain, Birkenhead, Curzon, Balfour, Horne, Derby, Lee of Fareham, Worthington-Evans, even Baldwin – seemed well content with Lloyd George's leadership, and with a government that was undeniably active and effective, if controversial.

As Bonar Law said to Balfour after the government had fallen, the Prime Minister's approach to domestic and foreign problems alike genuinely transcended party barriers. 'L.G.'s character and habit of mind made him approach any new problem in a spirit of complete detachment from traditional prejudices or principles. This made him absolutely impartial between the Parties which, for the head of a Coalition Government, was a great advantage.'[31] Not until Bonar Law re-emerged from retirement after illness, to play a somewhat ambiguous part as an independent supporter of the government from the end of 1921, did any Unionist stand out as a possible leader of the opposition. Until then, and indeed for several months thereafter, Unionists were as satisfied as Liberals were with the Prime Minister's conduct of affairs and his appeal to genuinely supra-party considerations. They accepted his view that the Coalition occupied a creative middle role between 'the revolutionary and the reactionary',[32] and that the major problems of the time (Bonar Law cited peace, housing, imperial preference, labour, pensions and Ireland)[33] necessitated a national approach, just as had the winning of the war. The Cabinet proudly declared in June 1920 that it existed to resist sectional pressures from capitalist and trade unionist alike, whether for punitive wage reductions or for an equally punitive capital levy.[34]

The 'unity' of wartime was frequently cited on coalition platforms as a major precedent for sustaining the government now. The 'unity of command' between Haig and Foch was the model, so men like Hilton Young or Lord Derby argued, for the union between the coalition armies.[35] And, in any case, there was something else binding Unionists and Liberals together – an overriding fear of organised labour. The tide of trade union militancy from the national railway strike of September–October 1919 to 'Black Friday' and the defeat of the Triple Alliance in April 1921; the pressure for 'direct action' seen in the unions' campaign to stop the sending of arms to Poland; above all, the ideology of Bolshevism with which labour leaders such as Arthur Cook ('a humble follower of Lenin') declared unwise sympathy – all these bound together the enemies of labour into apprehensive unity. Lloyd George was indeed on firm ground in claiming that, whatever their other differences, Liberals and Unionists were as one in defending private enterprise and the basis of a free society. To this, Unionists could add the appeal for order and for discipline. The anti-Bolshevist card was above all others the one for Lloyd George to play. It was his greatest asset in keeping his peacetime coalition in being for so long.

The technical aspects of the management of the coalition in 1919–22 undoubtedly caused immense difficulties – ones that became more pressing as time went on. The Coalition, after all, was a merger of highly independent parties. The Liberal and Unionist supporters of the government in the house sat as separate parties, under separate leadership. As an additional complication, Lloyd George shrewdly declined the offer of the chairmanship of the Coalition Liberals. The parties were also separately whipped – the result of an insistence by the Coalition Liberals that if there were a joint coalition whip it would alienate some of the Liberals who had fought the election as supporters of Asquith. Law added, in vain, that 'this would be the greatest possible mistake from your [Lloyd George's] point of view and that what we should aim at is to treat the whole of the Coalition members as a homogeneous body with one Whip for all and with arrangements that they should not sit separately in the House.'[36] But the political realities were against him, and Liberals who backed the coalition continued to be whipped separately, first by Guest, then by McCurdy.

Co-operation in the constituencies was also immensely difficult to attain. The main problem here was, once again, the Coalition Liberals. At first, they were reluctant to fight Asquithian candidates in by-elections. Not until the débâcle of Spen Valley did they do so. Their candidate there, Colonel Fairfax, finished up humiliatingly at the bottom of the poll, local Liberals clearly having voted for the Wee Free candidate, Sir John Simon. More to the point, the Coalition Liberals simply had no election machinery; the official party was entirely in Asquithian hands, save only in Wales. This meant that, in Coalition Liberal seats which became vacant, there was virtually no local machine to uphold the coalition cause, and local Unionists had to do their best to plug the gap. In addition, government ministers and sometimes members of the prime minister's personal entourage or even family came to assist. But there was a limit to what the front bench and a Welsh Mafia could achieve. The fact that the Coalition Liberals had simply no grass-roots organisation was a powerful unbalancing factor within the coalition, and a constant source of friction. In Spen Valley, Dartford, South Norfolk and other places, all Coalition Liberal seats in 1918, local Liberal bodies chose Wee Free candidates. Walter Long emphasised how unfair this was to the Unionists; the steady loss of Coalition Liberal seats in by-elections was the result.[37] Conversely, when Unionist seats fell vacant, there was scant help that local Liberals were able or willing to give; usually local party workers supported the Wee Free or Labour candidate. In these circumstances, it was particularly galling for Younger, the Unionist party manager, to receive a protest from Freddie Guest about the reluctance of Paisley Unionists to fight Asquith in the by-election there. Even worse, Guest tried to get the Cabinet Organisation Committee to agree to transfer some Scottish seats from Unionist to Liberal hands at the next election.[38]

By-elections, then, were a constant problem for the coalition. They reflected the fact that it was less a coalition between one party and another than one between a party and a prime minister whose party resources, outside his native land, were minimal. It was not surprising at all that by January 1922 Younger had become an influential voice of protest against the government's strategy. When he denounced in the press the premier's secret intention of holding a general election soon after the Anglo–French conference at Cannes, his position was too powerful for him to be deposed. The Unionist party machine, smarting at years of unhappy relations with its Coalition Liberal allies, was turning decisively against the coalition which it believed it had created.

Finance and patronage created another nagging problem for the coalition. Here, too, the difficulty was the same. Just as the Coalition Liberals had no organisation, so they had no funds. Lloyd George had, therefore, to acquire them somehow, and he did so by means of soliciting gifts, often through the sale of peerages and knighthoods through the Rabelaisian mediation of 'Bronco Bill' Sutherland in London's clubland. This was the origin of the notorious 'Lloyd George Fund' which did its architect such lasting harm. The difficulties for the Unionists, however, arose as much from practical as from moral objections. Certainly, many strait-laced Conservatives felt that Lloyd George's peers and 'dreadful knights' derived from a lower social stratum and were selected on a more obviously cash basis than was customary. But Unionists also had offered peerages in return for contributions to party funds, and had done so for decades. The difficulty in 1919–22 lay in determining which nominee would appear on which party's honours list, and how the proceeds would then be allocated. Younger claimed bitterly in early 1921 that 'Freddie is poaching our men',[39] and that it was Liberal and not Unionist coffers that were benefiting from the transactions of the whips. Much of the later outcry against Lloyd George's financial negotiations in building up a party political fund, the public dismay at the quality of Sir Joseph Robinson and other proposed peers, seems hypocritical. But there can be no doubt that difficulties of financial management must be added to the many tensions disturbing the coalition. They underlined its unnatural, wartime origins.

The one way of solving the problems at a stroke and extending the coalition's life almost indefinitely would have been by turning a coalition government into a coalition party. From the autumn of 1919 onwards, Lloyd George was bent on 'fusion', a nation-wide merger of the coalition parties. He devoted his efforts to persuading his Liberal government colleagues that the old party labels were meaningless and that only a fusion of the anti-socialist parties could cope adequately with the problems of the time, especially the challenge of Bolshevism.[40] Two Liberals supported him with enthusiasm. Addison saw a national government as the only instrument for dealing effectively with social reform on a radical basis. Churchill, conversely, wanted a coalition government to fight the menace of Bolshevism and of a Labour Party that was 'unfit to govern'. The Unionists were more circumspect. Bonar Law went along reluctantly with Lloyd George's plans. Birkenhead was much more enthusiastic, as he had been in 1910, and trumpeted the cause of a national government in the Rothermere press. Garvin and other conservative editors were also strongly in favour. But between 16 and 18 March 1920 fusion collapsed. It was a crucial moment – the beginning of the end of Lloyd George's dream of permanent coalition. Thereafter, some kind of Tory rebellion against the constraints of coalition seems in retrospect to have been inevitable. Oddly enough, the immediate difficulty came from the Coalition Liberals, who might have been thought to have had every incentive for ensuring their own future by merging with the more powerful Unionists. The problem was that the Coalition Liberals maintained that they were still Liberals, that over free trade, social reform, foreign policy and other questions a vital gulf still divided them from the Unionist mind. Baffled by the resistance he met at a meeting of Liberal Cabinet ministers on 16 March, Lloyd George had to retreat. He altered his prearranged plea for fusion when he met the Coalition Liberal backbenchers two days later. Instead, he put merely an anti-climactic case for 'closer co-operation' with the Unionists in the constituencies, lacing his speech with anti-Bolshevik rhetoric that lent itself to easy ridicule by Lady Violet Bonham-Carter and other opponents. Since the Liberals would not be wooed into fusion, the Unionists obviously would not put themselves out for so unattractive a prize. Bonar Law and Chamberlain viewed the end of fusion with total equanimity; Law told Balfour that 'it had been more necessary from L.G.'s point of view than ours'.[41] Fusion, then, was dead. Nothing like it was seriously proposed again. Indeed, by early 1922 there were renewed probes by backbenchers on both sides about a possible reunion of Asquithian and Coalition Liberals. These were relatively minor worries for the harassed and desperately tired prime minister. But they heralded the gradual but inevitable demise of the coalition which he led.

It may in retrospect seem surprising that the coalition hung on for so long, and that it was not until 19 October 1922, after the back-bench Unionist 'revolt' against their leaders at the Carlton Club meeting, that the government eventually fell. The reasons for the success of the coalition's remaining in office for four years raise far wider questions than are relevant here. It may be remarked that the government, especially in the spheres of disarmament and foreign policy, was far from ineffective. Most of its policies seemed to command a consensus of national support. Skilful tacking prevented an undue movement either to left or to right. If there were the Irish treaty and anti-unemployment policies to please Liberals, there were anti-Waste and the Geddes economies for the Unionists. As the furore over Genoa petered out, the government still seemed secure in office. Unionist back-bench protests were as ineffective as ever. Chamberlain, Horne and Birkenhead formed a kind of 'inner Cabinet', along with Churchill, bound in fealty to the prime minister. The next election still appeared certain to be fought on a coalition basis, with perhaps somewhat different terms negotiated by the various parties from those of 1918.

But there was another, more directly relevant, reason for the perpetuation of the coalition government. It was that the only feasible alternative also appeared to be some kind of coalition – probably an alliance of the Asquithian Liberals with the more moderate elements in the Labour Party, as advocated by Massingham in the *Nation*.[42] Lloyd George probably reflected the generally agreed view when he declared that some kind of coalition for Britain was inevitable, and that opinions differed only as to the appropriate mix. Another opposition group, those paternalist centrists, mainly of Anglican persuasion, associated with Lord Robert Cecil, were also, in essence, anti-government coalitionists. Mainly Unionists, their saviour, oddly enough, was the Liberal Lord Grey, a somewhat reluctant and elusive Messiah.[43] On the whole, Lloyd George's brand of coalition seemed more convincing and plausible than either of these possibilities. Unless the very idea of coalition could be undermined by the effective revival of party, Lloyd George would remain in office. Of course, there was Labour, steadily growing in strength and self-confidence, but still largely a political front for the trade unions (now losing members in the aftermath of the industrial recession) rather than an organised and coherent party. For most middle-class voters, almost any kind of national government was preferable to the unknown terrors of MacDonald and his red hordes. Unionist unrest over the coalition was still safely contained as the House went into recess in the summer of 1922. Sutherland confidently assured Lloyd George that Younger found his supporters only in seats where Central Office paid the election expenses, plus a few genuine die-hards like Page Croft, Gretton and Rupert Gwynne. At the Constitutional Club, Younger had been denounced for manifold crimes including 'the making of bad beer & selling it in the most miserable tied houses in the trade'. 'The Prime Minister's friends', Sutherland portentously concluded, 'regard the Prime Minister as being in a strong position.'[44]

Six weeks later, Lloyd George was out of office for ever. The reasons for the downfall of his coalition on 19 October 1922 lie in long-term political, social and ideological factors which must be explored on another occasion.[45] In a general sense, Lloyd George's fall reflected the fact that the national imperatives of wartime had given way to the sectional pressures of a new world in which party again held a central place. This can be linked, in turn, to changes in class alignments and in the economic structure between 1918 and 1922. The crisis over Greek–Turkish relations and the threat of war with Kemal's Turks at Chanak was the occasion rather than the cause of the government's downfall. In terms of Lloyd George's government as a species of coalition, Chanak showed how one decisive crisis could magnify and exaggerate all the weaknesses inherent in the government – as they had done since the failure of 'fusion' in March 1920. In an ultimate crisis, Lloyd George had nothing on which to rely. Unionists, weary of long years of frustration and badgering over by-election arrangements and patronage (now a wasting asset as the government's time ran out), fled from the government like lemmings. Backbenchers, under-secretaries, Cabinet ministers like Baldwin and Griffith-Boscawen joined in the rush. At the appropriate eleventh hour, with exquisite style and timing, the august figure of Curzon joined them (if 'joined' be not too committed a term). Bonar Law, though, was obviously the predestined leader and symbol of the Unionist revolt. Baffled at the level of party and of parliament, Lloyd George could find few allies at the executive level either. Most of the imperial nations were either apathetic or hostile over Chanak. Only New Zealand and Newfoundland offered token support, for what it was worth. Abroad, a chaotic Italy clearly could not help, while in France Poincaré was openly siding with the Turks and even urging them to think of acquiring Eastern Thrace on the European mainland. In Britain, Labour would fight no more wars for Lloyd George, not for the Straits or any other ostensible cause, and murmured threats of 'direct action'. Elsewhere, Keynes's famous assaults on the peace treaties, and their alleged economic consequences, had fuelled a national mood of isolationism. The British, once guardians of the *Pax Britannica*, now felt little pride in acting (to quote Bonar Law) 'alone as policemen of the world'.[46] There was therefore no significant element anywhere on which Lloyd George could rely – save for his own bewildered and demoralised Coalition Liberals whom he had treated with contempt for many months, but now his only remaining cadre of supporters. Contrary to his own avowals for many years, he did indeed appear to be turning into another Peel – if indeed he did not become another Joseph Chamberlain, cut off from his radical roots. Politically, as well as militarily, the war had ended for Lloyd George. So had the 'national' mood on which he had traded for so long. The mighty coalition, so dominant over the 'cabin boys', Younger and their like, a few months back, had vanished with the autumn leaves. It was one with Tyre and Nineveh, and no less irrelevant.

In 1922, unlike 1945, the idea of coalition was much discredited. Indeed, for years afterwards, left and right agreed in using the Lloyd George coalition of 1918–22 as a convenient scapegoat for all the ills from which Britain laboured. For the left, the coalition had been a time of class war, of the Sankey betrayal, of Black Friday, of anti-Bolshevism run mad, with the Black and Tans in Ireland and the White Russians in the east as its mercenaries. For the right, the coalition had been a time of opportunism and dishonesty, of adventures in foreign policy and corruption at home, with the Lloyd George Fund symbolising the free-wheeling habits of the late premier and his presidential style. Some echoes of coalitions were still heard in the land.

Throughout the 1923 parliament, the 'National Liberals' were, in Trevor Wilson's illuminating phrase, 'coalitionists in a post-coalition world'.[47] The shotgun marriage of Lloyd George and Asquith in November 1923 (followed by repentance at scant leisure) ended all that. In any case, most of the leading 'Coaly Libs' found their natural habitat by moving to the right: Greenwood, Guest, Hilton Young, Grigg, Mond and, of course, Churchill all took this route. Addison was a rare, and distinguished, defector to Labour. He served with authority under MacDonald in 1929–31 and under Attlee in 1945–51 where he could digress before his Cabinet colleagues on the ills of coalitionism after the previous war.[48] On the Unionist side, the big guns of the party, Chamberlain, Horne, Balfour, Birkenhead, Lee of Fareham and others, largely remained aloof from Bonar Law and Baldwin's Conservative governments of 1922 and 1923. They were still faithful to the coalition memories of yesteryear. In May 1923, however, there was something of a break in ranks when Worthington-Evans left to serve under Baldwin.[49] After the December 1923 general election, all Conservatives were united again, with the first Labour government having lent their unity added fervour. Now, indeed, was the time for all good men to come to the aid of the capitalist system.

The coalition government, then, passed unlamented. Politics after 1922 were largely a reaction against it, and especially against its former leader, now a distrusted figure. With hindsight, the record of the coalition may not seem so ignoble. It pursued far-sighted policies of social reform and reconciliation. The survival of democratic institutions in Britain during the inter-war years perhaps owes something to its efforts. But in the revived world of party, polarised by the class confrontation of capital and labour, that was not the way that men in the twenties saw things at all, and they were probably right. The coalition, from a technical standpoint, may be seen to have had basic structural weaknesses. The relations between the major parties within it were never cordial. Differences over whipping or patronage would become gaping divisions. By 1922 the composition of the government was too one-sided. It depended to an undue extent on the dominance of the executive over the legislative, fuelled by the needs of national recovery. Again, between 1919 and 1922 there had been a real and growing opposition, the Labour Party, and a kind of basic challenge to the government that Churchill had never experienced in 1940–5. During the wartime period, Lloyd George's government had transcended, or just ignored, peripheral attacks of this kind. In peacetime, with party again becoming an essential part of the 'normalcy' of post-war life, they were increasingly decisive. Ultimately, though, the roots of the fall of the coalition of 1918–22 lie not in technical considerations of machine management but in wider factors. The government depended in January 1919 on three things – on an agreed programme of priorities, on a leader, and on a mood. Long before October 1922, they were all under challenge. The manifesto of 1918 was forgotten or betrayed; Lloyd George had long been whittled down to human size; the national euphoria of wartime was out of date. In such circumstances, the coalition had no purpose.

There is a postscript to all this. The heirs of the political revolution of 1922 were Stanley Baldwin and Ramsay MacDonald. They symbolised the new revived decencies of party – respectable Conservatism and constitutional Labour – after the adventures of the Lloyd George era. Each of them represented a reaction to the coalition. Baldwin had been foremost amongst those ministerial rebels against the government at the Carlton Club. What good Tory would ever forget his attack on the prime minister as 'a dynamic force' who might split the Unionist Party as fatally as he had already split the Liberal Party? MacDonald, the very epitome of anti-war protest, inherited the mantle of idealism and conscience on the left. He was the natural leader of the new progressivism, committed to social change and to international reconciliation after 1922.[50] Throughout the twenties, Baldwin and MacDonald based their careers not so much on their differences from each other as on the gulf that divided them from Lloyd George and the coalition. In the 1929 election, they each attacked Lloyd George's Orange Book and the Keynesian schemes for tackling unemployment through public works projects, more vehemently than they assailed each other. And yet it is the supreme irony of our century that these two men, whose very roles depended on their being honourable alternatives to coalition, were themselves to be the architects of a new 'national' venture. In August 1931, many of the arguments against coalition that had been advanced in 1922 could have been put even more forcibly. The Labour Party was far more fractionalised now than the Liberals had been in 1918, and the government's claim to be truly 'national' was all the more unreal. The days of August 1931 were even less appropriate a time for looking calmly at the realities of coalitionism than were those of December 1916. For all that, Baldwin and MacDonald pursued the mirage of 'national unity' as fervently as they had denounced it in 1922, and the government described in the next chapter was the result. For this reason alone, the historian may well conclude that the roots of coalitions lie not in the immutable forms of political structures or in the composition of a decision-making élite but in the fluctuations of historical circumstance. One man's 'national unity' is another's 'opportunism'. One man's 'petty partisanship' is another's 'principled independence'. The rhetoric, from the days of Rosebery to those of Heath, remains much the same. It is coalitions that come and go. Doubtless they will always do so, as long as Britain remains a nation capable of unity at all.

# 3 1924–1932

## DAVID MARQUAND

'Coalitions are detestable, are dishonest', Ramsay MacDonald told a packed House of Commons in his first speech as Prime Minister in February 1924: though his Government was in a minority, it would 'bring before this House proposals to deal with great national and international problems, and we are not afraid of what fate we may meet in the process'.[1] There were to be no deals or accommodations, overt or covert. Lacking a majority, Labour could not carry through socialist measures, and it would not try: the notion that it should deliberately ride for a fall, by introducing a socialist King's Speech against which the opposition parties would be obliged to combine, so as to force a general election which would have to be fought on its own distinctive programme, found favour only with a minority on the Left of the party, and there is no evidence that the leadership had even considered it. But although the new Government recognised that its minority status placed severe limits on its freedom of action, it intended, within those limits, to behave as though it had a majority. By a quirk of fate, Labour had suddenly been given an opportunity to show that a working-class party could carry on the King's Government as competently as the older parties could. It did not intend to weaken the effect of that demonstration by appearing to accept a second-class status. The new Labour Ministers were to be proper ministers, judging for themselves what was necessary in the national interest, and submitting their judgements to Parliament without prior consultation with any other party. If they were defeated on a vote of confidence, they would go to the country. Otherwise, they would conduct the country's business by the normal rules.

That was the message of MacDonald's speech; and that was what happened in practice. Labour would not have been able to take office in the first place without Liberal acquiescence. But the Liberals got nothing in return. In a celebrated speech a month before MacDonald kissed hands, Asquith had boasted that, no matter who held office, 'it is we, if we really understand our business, who really control the situation'. His boast was justified by the arithmetic of the House of Commons, but that, in itself, made it all the more necessary for the Labour Party to behave as though it were not. Asquith and his

52

followers were kept at arm's length. No deals were made, and it is unlikely that any were contemplated. In March 1924 Wheatley brought in an uncharacteristically ill-judged bill to prohibit evictions in cases where the non-payment of rent was due to unemployment. The bill was defeated, and the Government then threw its weight behind a Liberal private member's bill instead. But there is no evidence that it did so in response to Liberal pressure or after consultation with the Liberal party. Soon afterwards, Snowden introduced a budget cast in a classically Liberal mould. But here, too, there is no evidence of direct Liberal influence. In May the Liberals saved the government's skin by voting against a Conservative motion to reduce the Minister of Labour's salary. But they did so because they were afraid of a general election, not because they had made an agreement with the government. Not surprisingly, the Liberals became increasingly exasperated with this state of affairs. By September it was clear that they would vote against the government's Russian treaty even if this meant bringing the government down; in October the government fell, on Asquith's motion to set up a select committee on the Campbell case. For the historian of coalitions, the 1924 government is, in short, a non-event.

It is, however, an instructive non-event. The forces which kept the Liberal and Labour parties apart in 1924 were still in operation five years later; some of them are still in operation today. The first and most obvious was that the Liberal and Labour parties were competitors for the same constituency. Eighteen months before becoming Prime Minister, MacDonald had proclaimed defiantly that in Britain, 'we shall always tend to return to two great parties and that is the position today. The two parties fighting for supremacy are our own and the Tory Party of reaction'.[2] As he knew better than most, that was aspiration, not reality. The Liberals were far from being a spent force in the early 1920s. The Labour Party came ahead of them in 1922 and again in 1923, but not by much. It was far from certain that it would continue to come ahead of them in future. Thanks to the upsurge in trade union membership which had taken place during and after the war, and the extension in the suffrage which had been made at the end of the war, the Labour Party now had a much bigger electoral base than it had had before 1914. But its base was not yet big enough to make it, without question, the main anti-Conservative party in the country. If British politics really were to revolve around a struggle between the Labour Party and the 'Tory Party of reaction', a large number of people who had formerly voted Liberal in the past, and who still thought of themselves as Liberals, would have to be persuaded to vote Labour instead. If they were to be so persuaded, they would have to be convinced that the Liberal party could no longer influence events, and that the Labour Party was now the most effective custodian of the Liberal tradition. Hence MacDonald's lordly, not to say cavalier, attitude to the Liberals, whose votes could have brought him down at almost any moment. If he allowed the government to look as though it depended on the Liberals, he would not only strengthen their credibility; he would weaken Labour's credibility as well. He had to prove that he could govern without the Liberals, and he could only do that if he behaved as though he did not care whether they voted against him or not.

That was only part of the story. By 1924, the Labour Party had been a significant parliamentary force for a total of eighteen years. It had become one in the first place only because its leaders had made a secret electoral pact with the Liberal chief whip. For four years it had helped to maintain a minority Liberal government in office. For three, Labour ministers had taken part in coalition governments, not only with Liberals, but with Conservatives as well. But past practice was one thing: attitude and ideology another. Though few British socialists consciously accepted the Marxist doctrine of the class war, most took it for granted that the interests of the 'workers by hand and brain' were irreconcilably opposed to the interests of all other classes in society, and that those interests could be fully secured only when the means of production were socially owned. The 'workers by hand and brain' were at last beginning to recognise where their true interests lay and to throw off the capitalist yoke: the Labour Party's job was to encourage them in that process. It could only do that if it turned its face like flint against both the capitalist parties. For the central assumption on which its claim to power was based was that capitalism was capitalism and socialism was socialism: that the ills of capitalism could be fully cured only by socialism and that 'palliatives' that fell short of socialism could only make the disease worse than it was already. If that assumption were valid, there was no room for honest co-operation between the Labour Party and either of the two capitalist parties. If the Labour Party nevertheless engaged in such co-operation it would deny what most party members saw as its fundamental purpose.

Alongside these attitudes ran a deeper current of feeling, harder to describe but as important to identify, which probably had an even greater effect on the party's behaviour. Then, even more than now, the Labour Party was the party of the 'outs' looking in: the party of provincials, ill-at-ease in the metropolis: the party of suburban villas and pokey bed-sitting-rooms which had suddenly (and to its own surprise) burst in on a political world shaped by the assumptions of the country house and the London club. To be sure, it contained a number of upper-class and middle-class recruits. Eight out of the twenty members of MacDonald's first Cabinet had aristocratic or upper middle-class backgrounds. But the leading figures – the men who held the levers of party power and who commanded the allegiance of the rank and file – were all working-class in origin. So were 70 per cent of the Parliamentary Labour Party as a whole, and the overwhelming majority of party activists outside parliament. Of the 30 per cent of party members whose origins were not working-class, moreover, only a tiny handful came from the traditional ruling-class stable of public school, followed by Oxford or Cambridge.[3] Party feeling had often run high in the nineteenth and early twentieth centuries, and there had often been times when differences of ideology had coincided with differences of economic interest. But there had never been a time before when a major political party had belonged, so completely and so obviously, to a different social world from that of its rivals. And although it would be difficult to show that the social composition of the Parliamentary Labour Party had much effect on the party's policies, there can be little doubt that it had an immense effect on the party's attitudes to the older parties. Labour M.P.s were like nervous explorers in a hostile continent. They knew that they might, at any moment, be ambushed by the natives. They knew too that the most dangerous natives were those who appeared, at first sight, to be the most friendly. When the country was at war, as in 1915 or 1940, they were prepared to lower their guard. At other times, they assumed that safety lay in isolation.

All this was as true in 1929 as it had been in 1924. Indeed the attitudes which had led the 1924 government to keep the Liberals at arm's length were, if anything, reinforced by the experience of the intervening five years. The fact that it had fallen on a Liberal motion was seen, in Labour circles, as a final proof that the Liberals were, at best, Conservatives in disguise. The 'red letter' election that followed seemed to show yet again that the capitalist parties would stop at nothing to do down the working class. The menacing upsurge in Liberal activity which followed Lloyd George's succession to the Liberal leadership in 1926, and the still more menacing improvement in the Liberals' by-election performances which accompanied it, showed that Labour's position as the main anti-Conservative party in the state was still far from impregnable, and that the Liberals were still capable of mounting a serious challenge to it. In the end, of course, the Liberals did much less well in 1929 than they had done in 1923, while Labour did better. But there was no way of knowing that this would happen before the votes were counted. Between 1926 and 1929 the Liberal Party was perceived, by most of the leading figures in the Labour Party, as a serious threat. In terms of ideas, if not in terms of votes, the perception was correct. And although it is often forgotten, votes are sometimes swung by ideas.

In spite of this, the second Labour government followed a very different course from the first. Between June and December 1929, the Liberals were treated with the same lordly disdain which had been meted out to them in 1924. Lloyd George's attempt to persuade the government to rewrite its bill reorganising the coal industry to take account of the Liberal policy of compulsory amalgamation was rebuffed. Though he delivered a stinging attack on the bill in the second reading debate, the government won the day with the help of two Liberal votes and a number of Liberal abstentions. But lordly disdain was only feasible while the electoral omens were propitious from the government's point of view, and they did not remain propitious for long. By the early months of 1930, the government was beginning to run out of electoral steam, as the effects of the great depression began to make themselves felt. In a by-election in February 1930, the Labour majority at Sheffield, Brightside, fell from 10,349 to 2931. At the beginning of May, Labour lost West Fulham to the Conservatives; at the end of the month, the Conservatives increased their majority at Central Nottingham from 2998 to 7023. Figures like these spoke louder than Labour's tradition of political exclusiveness, louder even than its long-term interest in destroying the Liberal Party as a serious force. At the beginning of February 1930 MacDonald noted in his diary that Lloyd George had 'talked with Thomas, Snowden, Henderson and myself about an agreement to keep us in office for from two to three years. Turned upon whether we would give him a bargain on Electoral Reform.'[4] Six weeks later he noted that a similar group of ministers had decided 'with only myself unwilling to tell Liberals we would introduce an electoral reform bill if we remain in office'.[5]

For the Liberals, it was a false dawn. In the middle of May 1930, the Labour Party executive instructed the Labour representatives on the three-party Ullswater conference – which had been set up in December 1929, to inquire into the law governing parliamentary elections – to vote against changes in the electoral system. But although the prospect of a deal on the electoral system receded into the background during the next few months, the forces which had made it a possibility continued to gather strength. By an odd coincidence, Sir Oswald Mosley resigned from the government in protest against the Cabinet's unwillingness to adopt his famous memorandum on unemployment on the same day that the Labour Party executive decided against electoral reform. In the confusion that followed his resignation, it looked for a while as though a Liberal–Labour agreement might be reached by the high road of policy accommodation instead of by the low road of parliamentary manoeuvre. Partly because he wanted to defuse opposition charges of inactivity, partly because he genuinely believed that party co-operation was needed to solve the country's problems, MacDonald issued an invitation to Baldwin and Lloyd George to confer with the Government on the economic crisis. Baldwin refused, but Lloyd George accepted; and during the summer of 1930 a series of two-party conferences took place at which Liberal 'experts' vainly tried to persuade the ministers and officials concerned to adopt the Liberal policy of a massive road programme, financed by a development loan.

The talks soon ran into the sand. The two departments mainly affected – the Treasury and the Ministry of Transport – were both passionately opposed to the Liberal policy. Lloyd George knew in his bones that they were wrong, but only in his bones: he lacked the economic knowledge to disprove the assumptions on which their arguments were based. By late September he was falling back on the charge that the government lacked 'drive' – a charge which, as MacDonald happily pointed out to the Cabinet, amounted to a back-handed admission that there was no alternative to the government's policy after all. But the Liberals were not to be put off by intellectual reverses. The high road having failed them, they returned to the low road – Sir Herbert Samuel telling MacDonald that they would be prepared, on suitable terms, to keep the government in office for two years, and Lloyd George warning that, unless the government brought in either proportional representation or the alternative vote, they would be obliged to turn it out. After a long discussion, the Cabinet decided that Lloyd George should be told that the government was prepared to consider the alternative vote, and that if it reached agreement with the Liberals it would try to persuade the Labour Party executive and annual conference to support the alternative vote as well.

What happened next is far from clear. Under pressure from the Liberals, the Cabinet decided that the King's Speech at the beginning of the new parliamentary session should contain a commitment to electoral reform. The nature of the reform was not specified, however, and in his speech in the debate on the address MacDonald carefully left it uncertain whether the Government intended to change the electoral system or merely to make minor reforms in electoral law. As late as 17 November 1930 a Cabinet discussion on relations with the Liberals, in which a number of ministers drew attention to the need to get a 'timely' expression of the Liberals' views on projected legislation, ended with the conclusion that nothing could be done without an agreement on electoral reform, on which the Cabinet had not yet made up its mind.[6] Next day, however, MacDonald recorded another conversation with Lloyd George in which: 'Lloyd George, Samuel, Henderson and myself discussed co-operation to give the Government security. One of the counters being Alternative Vote.'[7] In mid-December 1930 the Labour Party executive —having first received an assurance from Henderson that the government had made no pact with the Liberals – voted by 16 to 3 for a resolution supporting the inclusion of the alternative vote in the Electoral Reform Bill. Next day, a joint meeting of the executive and the parliamentary party passed a similar resolution by 133 votes to 20. At the beginning of February 1931 the second reading of the Electoral Reform Bill – duly incorporating the alternative vote – was carried by a majority of 65.

Henderson's assurance to the National Executive was clearly false in spirit, but it was probably true in the letter. Though the details of the transaction are not known, the evidence suggests that what had been made with the Liberals was less a treaty than an entente, the terms of which were not wholly clear and the existence of which could be disavowed by either party if the need arose. At a meeting of the Liberal Candidates' Association at the beginning of December 1930, Lloyd George denied that he and his colleagues had made any pact with the government, and insisted that the Liberals should keep up their pressure on ministers, if necessary to the point of inflicting defeats on them. This was not an idle threat. Only a few days after the Electoral Reform Bill received its second reading, the Cabinet was forced by the threat of a defeat in the division lobby to accept a Liberal motion calling for an independent committee to advise the Chancellor of the Exchequer on the best way to make economies in government expenditure – a portentous concession, which led directly to the establishment of the May Committee, and hence to the May Report which helped to cause the confidence crisis of August 1931. Soon after that, the Liberals joined forces with the Conservatives to carry what amounted to a wrecking amendment to the Government's bill repealing the hated 1927 Trade Disputes Act. In June 1931 the Liberals revolted against the land-tax clauses of Snowden's Finance Bill – forcing the government to choose between what Snowden, at any rate, considered to be a humiliating surrender, and a defeat which might have led to a general election.

In spite of occasional upsets, however, the entente gradually became more comprehensive in scope and more solid in character. The Liberals stopped insisting on the development loan as the cure for all ills. Ministers became receptive to Liberal ideas, or at any rate more polite to their proponents. From the end of March 1931 regular meetings took place between the leading figures on both sides, designed, as MacDonald put it in a letter to Lloyd George, to 'enable me to see how things are going generally from your point of view and . . . enable me to concentrate my attention on the various points of weakness.'[8] Joint committees were set up to consider such matters as telephone development, town planning and the housing of farm labourers; through these, Liberal advisers were slowly enmeshed into the government machine. In the middle of April 1931 Lloyd George led 30 Liberals into the government lobby in a division on a Conservative motion censuring its unemployment policy. Most remarkable of all, he dictated a memorandum to his secretary in July 1931, recording a conversation with MacDonald in which MacDonald had said that the Labour Party wanted an 'alliance' with the Liberals and that he hoped that Lloyd George would join the government as Foreign Secretary or Chancellor of the Exchequer.[9]

The status of this conversation is obscure, and it would be a mistake to read too much into it. All the same, it is a revealing indication of the character of Liberal–Labour relations in the summer of 1931. The two parties still differed profoundly in ideology and social composition: the partnership between them was based less on positive enthusiasm than on fear of the alternative. But marriages of convenience often work, and for the best part of six months theirs had worked better than either would have been entirely happy to admit. It was not a coalition, but it was certainly a quasi-coalition. The Liberals had no ministers in the government and were not bound by the ties of collective responsibility. On the other hand, they were keeping the government in office and were known to be keeping the government in office. In an area of critical importance to themselves, they had forced a fundamental change in government policy; as time had gone on, their influence on other areas of policy had grown, and so had their willingness to be identified with the government in the public eye. At a deeper level, moreover, the prospect of electoral reform had removed the main conflict of interest which had divided the two parties in the past. As MacDonald had seen all along, electoral reform would perpetuate the three-party system: that was why he had been against it. Now that it had been conceded, however, a return to 'two great parties' — his old objective of the early 1920s – was no longer feasible, and there was no longer any need to make the destruction of the Liberal Party Labour's central priority. In the harsh, winner-take-all system of classical, single-member constituencies, the struggle between the Liberal and Labour parties was bound to be a struggle to the death. Under the alternative vote they would have been able to fight with the gloves on. The arrangement between the Liberal and Labour parties was, of course, inherently unstable: arrangements between rival political parties usually are. But although its life was short, it is hard to argue that it was more unstable than it would have been if it had been a full-scale coalition.

The quasi-coalition of early 1931 was the product of months of manoeuvre and negotiation. The real coalition for which 1931 is famous was the product of a last-minute change of mind on the part of its head. It is true that MacDonald had shown a fleeting sympathy for the idea of a National Government nine months before. In late October and November 1930, the Labour Government's manifest inability to find solutions for the depression, and an anxious awareness among the independent-minded in all three parties that no solution was likely to emerge from the rituals of party warfare, had provoked a flood of dinner-table gossip about the need for an all-party government to save the situation. Lloyd George, an inveterate coalitionist in times of crisis, had supported the idea in private. J. L. Garvin, the editor of the *Observer* had campaigned for it publicly, in a series of apocalyptic editorials. Partly because he had become increasingly exasperated with the divisions in his Cabinet, partly because he suspected that there was a move on foot to replace him as party leader, MacDonald had toyed with the idea as well; and at the beginning of December 1930 he had even mentioned it to Baldwin. When Baldwin had shown that it had no attractions for him, however, MacDonald had swiftly retreated; and it seems clear that he had seen it as, at most, a vague and uncertain option to be left open for the future, not as a real possibility for the present.

When it became a real possibility in August 1931, his first instinct was to shy away. In the most disastrous blunder of his life, he rejected Keynes's advice to devalue sterling, and fought with stubborn passion for cuts in spending on unemployment benefit large enough to balance the budget in the way that the Treasury and Bank of England thought essential to save the parity. But although this could reasonably be described as a coalition policy, there is no evidence that he wanted a coalition Government to carry it out. The Labour Government's death warrant was signed in the evening of 20 August, when a deputation from the TUC General Council made it clear that it would accept no cut in spending on the unemployed. On 21 August the Cabinet agreed to an economy programme of £56 million – £22 million less than the figure which had been unanimously agreed by the Cabinet economy committee three days before – but refused to make any cut in unemployment benefit. The Bank of England made it clear that this figure was too small to stop the drain of sterling; that evening, Neville Chamberlain and Sir Herbert Samuel, who were deputising for their respective party leaders, told MacDonald that if he wished to form a government with their co-operation, they would be prepared to serve under him. So far from accepting their offer MacDonald spent most of 22 and 23 August in a desperate attempt to persuade his colleagues to raise their bid by £20 millions – £12.5 millions of it to come from a cut in unemployment benefit of 10 per cent. He did not give up until the evening of 23 August, when it became clear that the Cabinet was split beyond repair. At lunchtime on 23 August, moreover, he explicitly decided not to form a National Government if the Labour Government should fall, on the grounds that if he did so he would 'face the whole antagonism of the Labour movt.'. Instead, he planned to leave office with his colleagues, and support the cuts he believed to be necessary from the Opposition benches below the gangway.[10] He did not begin to waver until that evening, and did not change his mind until the following morning.

It is true that his final decision was logically consistent with, perhaps even logically implied by, the stand he had taken ever since the crisis broke. From the beginning, he had been convinced that a forced devaluation would be a disaster for the country, and that it was his duty to do all he could to avoid it. On the altar of that conviction, he had been prepared to sacrifice, first the unity of the Labour Party, and then his own position as its leader. Having been so prepared, it was difficult for him to resist the argument that the surest way to avoid a forced devaluation was to form a National Government, and impossible to resist the conclusion that, in that case, it was his duty to form one. But although that logic was implicit in his actions from the first, it did not become apparent to him until the last moment. The scars left by the formation of the National Government lingered so long that it is hard, even now, to appreciate how close-run a thing it was. The fact remains that it came into existence only because, in the morning of 24 August, MacDonald reluctantly abandoned the view he had formed the day before, and adopted the King's view instead.

It is doubtful if either of his new allies had much more enthusiasm for the venture than he had. Chamberlain and Samuel had started to press him to form a National Government as soon as they discovered that the Labour Government was unlikely to make the cuts thought necessary by the Bank of England, and they continued to press for a National Government at every available opportunity thereafter. But although most Labour people, then and later, have assumed the contrary, it does not follow that they did so for reasons of party advantage. In reality, the Liberals and Conservatives both had more to lose from a National Government than they had to gain. It is true that the National Government gave the Liberals a badly-needed chance of office. It is also true that the whole episode dealt a shattering, though far from mortal, blow to the Liberal party. The Liberals did not know that this would happen, of course, but they would have had to be remarkably imperceptive not to realise that they might be putting their heads into a noose. The reason a National Government was on the cards at all was that the Labour Government was split. Almost by definition, therefore, the largest party in any National Government would be the Conservatives. On no plausible assumptions did the Liberals stand to gain more from an alliance with the Conservatives than from their existing alliance with the Labour Party. Thanks to Labour's electoral weakness, they had managed to bully the Labour Government into giving them at least the prospect of the alternative vote – a far more valuable prize, except in the shortest of short terms, than seats in the Cabinet. They had no realistic hope of repeating that performance with the Conservatives. For the Conservatives were not electorally weak. On the contrary, they were the favourites to win an election. They had no reason to fear Liberal threats and could snap their fingers if the Liberals tried to blackmail them.

The same applies to the Conservatives, though for rather different reasons. Before the crisis broke, Baldwin had been able to look forward, on any reasonable calculation of the odds, to returning to Downing Street within a year or two. The crisis had brought the prize much nearer, and the Labour government's inability to deal with the crisis brought it nearer still. If the Labour government fell, the alternative to a National Government would be a minority Conservative government, supported by the Liberals. In a National Government,

Baldwin could expect to be second-in-command. In a Conservative government, he would be prime minister. He was a strange man in many ways, but he was not strange enough to imagine that the second-in-command of a government headed by someone else could possibly be in a stronger position than the prime minister of government formed from his own party. Baldwin's personal interests were not, of course, identical with the interests of the Conservative party, but on this occasion there was little difference between them. Diehard, or apparently diehard, Conservatives, like Churchill or Amery, clearly stood to lose from a National Government; and although they cannot have been sure how much they were going to lose before the government was formed, they would have had to be remarkably imperceptive not to guess. Ambitious, middle-rank Conservatives must have realised that there would be less preferment for them in a coalition government than in a purely Conservative one. At a more elevated level, all Conservatives knew that they were well placed to win the next election on their own. If Labour left office in ignominy and disarray, to be followed by a minority Conservative government, an early election and a sweeping Conservative victory would both be almost certain. A National Government would, of course, split the Labour Party. But the Labour Party was split already, and the risk that it might close ranks in opposition was no greater than the risk that the Labour members of a National Government might rejoin their old colleagues when the crisis was over, and throw a mantle of respectability over the rest of the party. In the event, the Conservatives did well out of the National Government. Before it was formed, they had no way of knowing whether they would do well or badly. From their point of view, it was a bird in the bush. A minority Conservative government would have been a bird in the hand.

Like MacDonald himself, in short, the Conservatives and Liberals acted as they did because they believed that it was their duty to do so. Like him, they believed that a forced devaluation would be a disaster for the country. Like him, they believed that a National Government would be more likely to avoid that disaster than would a Conservative government dependent on Liberal support. They were party politicians, not saints. They did not want to damage their parties if they could help it, and when they thought it was safe to do so they pushed hard for their party interests. But they were also patriotic men, who wished to do the right thing by their country. Their behaviour in August 1931 only makes sense on the assumption that they believed themselves to be putting party second and country first. One of the reasons why they showed so much bitterness to the Labour Party thereafter is that they also believed that the Labour leaders who opposed the economy programme had done the opposite.

In a way they were right, though not in the way they imagined.

Henderson and the other Labour ministers who opposed cutting unemployment benefit took their stand on class loyalty, not on economic theory. They, too, believed that the parity had to be held and the budget balanced. But they did not believe that it was the Labour Party's job to penalise the unemployed in order to overcome a crisis which was none of their making. Still less did they believe that it was a Labour Government's job to break with the TUC and risk destroying the Labour movement. They were as patriotic as the Conservatives and Liberals, but they had a different view of patriotism. It was inconceivable to them that the country's interests could conflict with the interests of the class which they were in politics to represent: working people and their families *were* the country. When the experts told them that it would be fatal to leave the gold standard and that the budget would have to be balanced to stay on it, they acquiesced, for they lacked the economic knowledge to prove the experts wrong. When they were told that the national interest required them to balance the budget at the expense of the unemployed, they rebelled, for they could see that that must be wrong without economic knowledge. They had no alternative to offer, though they were later to acquire one, but that only made them more stubborn and resentful. Better do nothing than inflict extra hardships on the weakest of their people. If the crisis could be dealt with only by capitalist measures, let the capitalist parties apply them. Labour could then leave office with clean hands, and fight on in opposition for a better system.

British politics carried the scars of this conflict of perception for the next nine years. MacDonald had not wanted to form the government in the first place. Having agreed to do so in the end, he bent over backwards to prove that he had not been taken prisoner by his allies. Though it was clear from the beginning that it would depend overwhelmingly on Conservative votes, the Conservatives had only four places in a Cabinet of ten, as against two for the Liberals and four (including MacDonald's own) for the Labour Party. Outside the Cabinet, the Conservatives did better, with eight ministers of Cabinet rank out of 17 and nine junior ministers out of 16. But the Conservatives' edge in non-Cabinet posts was due largely to MacDonald's failure to persuade potential Labour ministers to follow him. Even in non-Cabinet posts, moreover, the Conservatives were nowhere near as strong as they were in the division lobbies. The Government's first parliamentary test came on 8 September 1931, when the House voted to resolve itself into a committee of ways and means. Of the 309 M.P.s who voted in the Government lobby, 243 were Conservatives. With them were 53 Liberals, 12 Labour men and three Independents. On those figures, the Conservatives were entitled to seven Cabinet posts instead of four, or to 31 ministerial offices altogether instead of 21. The new government's policies told the same story. In their discussions with MacDonald and

Snowden before the Labour government fell, the Conservatives had insisted on economies of around £100 million. In the end, the National Government's cuts totalled £70 million. The cut in unemployment benefit accounted for £13 million; almost the whole of the remainder had figured in the £56 million programme which had been accepted by the entire outgoing Cabinet. Judged by results, at any rate, if any prisoners had been taken, it was the Conservatives who had been taken prisoner by MacDonald.

That was not how things looked to MacDonald's old followers in the Labour Party. Before the Labour government fell, the arguments around the Cabinet table had concerned the government's response to the crisis: no one had disputed that the crisis was real. After the National Government took office, the preceding two weeks came to be seen in a more sinister light. Increasingly, Labour people came to believe the crisis had been a fraud – a 'bankers' ramp', which had been deliberately engineered to bring down the Labour government – and that MacDonald was either the tool or the accomplice of those who had perpetrated it. As these emotions gathered force, the party was swept further and further away from the position which its leaders had taken up in government. Not only the £76 million economy programme, which had been accepted by a majority of the Labour Cabinet, but the £56 million programme, which had been accepted by all of it, were rapidly forgotten. A few days after the National Government took office, the TUC General Council, the Labour Party executive and the consultative committee of the Parliamentary Labour Party published a joint manifesto, denouncing all the economies agreed upon by the outgoing Cabinet and advocating the quite different policy which had been advocated by the TUC. On 28 August a resolution approving the joint manifesto was carried by the Parliamentary Labour Party, with only a handful of dissentients. When Parliament debated the new government's National Economy Bill early in September, J. R. Clynes, who led for the opposition, came close to denying that the Labour Cabinet had agreed to any cuts at all, and argued that, in any case, its members were no longer bound by the decisions they had taken three weeks before.

The chief victim of Labour's change of tune was the Labour Party itself. When the National Government was formed, it had been agreed by all concerned that it would last for only a few weeks. The decision to set it up had been taken at a meeting between the King and the three party leaders at Buckingham Palace on 24 August. They had agreed, as Clive Wigram had recorded, afterwards, that as soon as it had passed 'an emergency bill or bills' to restore foreign confidence in sterling, the King would grant a dissolution. They had also agreed that, although it would remain in being during the election, each party would fight on its own lines. Privately, MacDonald had expected it to last 'about five weeks, to tide over the crisis', and had assumed that his own political career would end with it. As Labour's attacks on the government mounted in intensity, he began to have second thoughts. Why should he tamely leave office, pursued by howls of execration from his old followers? Would it not be better to remain in control of events, and be hanged for a sheep rather than for a lamb? In any case, was it really safe to have an election with the Labour Party in this mood? In a letter to Baldwin on 5 September he warned that the Labour Party had some 'rather detestable but nevertheless electorally effective cries . . . [If] it were to have a majority or could even form a Government after the next Election, the country would again be faced with a financial crisis which would then in all probability break upon it and ruin it.' The government, he conceded, could not outlast the immediate situation which had brought it into being. Was it really possible, however, 'to draw a line between this time of crisis and a normal condition which is to follow? I do not see any such line'.[11] Though he did not spell them out, the implications were clear. An early election might benefit the Labour Party. But the assumptions underlying the agreement to have an early election no longer held good. The obvious conclusion was that no election should be held after all, and that the government should stay in office instead.

It did not seem obvious to the Conservatives. They were now in one of their rare, but formidable, moods of crusading zeal. The country's problems, they believed, could be solved only by the historic Conservative policy of protection, which it was their mission to introduce. But protection was impossible without an election. When Chamberlain had tentatively raised the possibility of bringing in a revenue tariff in the new government's economy committee, Snowden had ruled it out without a discussion. In any case, there was no majority in the existing House of Commons. As the Conservatives saw it, the return of a protectionist majority at the earliest possible moment was not only a party interest, but a patriotic imperative. Besides, they had been promised an early election only a few days before. At the end of August, Baldwin had assured a meeting of Conservative M.P.s, peers and parliamentary candidates that they would have 'a straight fight on tariffs and against the Socialist party' as soon as the National Government's economies were passed.[12] His decision to serve under MacDonald had then been unanimously approved; though it would probably have been approved even if he had said nothing about an election, his followers would have a legitimate grievance if his assurance were subsequently forgotten. A few days after the meeting Lord Hailsham, who had moved the motion approving Baldwin's actions, published an article in the *Daily Express*, pointing out that the government had been formed for the 'one purpose' of balancing the budget, and insisting that as soon as that purpose had been achieved there should be 'an appeal to the country on the Conservative Party's constructive programme'.[13] As Baldwin knew better than most, the Conservatives had a short way with coalitions that appeared to endanger their party interests. He did not intend to let Hailsham do to him what he had done to the Conservative coalitionists in 1922.

On the other hand, MacDonald's warning that Labour's 'cries' might be 'electorally effective' seemed only too plausible. In the days before opinion polls, politicians had no way of knowing how the electorate had reacted to a sudden crisis, and in early September 1931 many politicians, on both sides of the House of Commons, assumed that Labour's campaign against the cuts was winning support in the country. More disquietingly still for would-be electioneers, it was beginning to look as if the financial crisis had not ended after all. Immediately after the National Government took office, confidence in sterling had recovered. But the recovery did not last, and by September withdrawals had resumed. One reason, the Bank believed, was that talk of an early election had been 'rather disturbing'.[14] Thus the Conservatives faced a dilemma which seemed likely to become increasingly painful as time went on. If they insisted on sticking to the Buckingham Palace agreement of 24 August, they might put Labour back in office, or provoke another sterling crisis, or both. If they followed MacDonald's line, and agreed that the National Government should stay in office after the budget had been balanced, the prospect of a tariff election and a protectionist majority would recede into an unforeseeable future.

The way out was found by Geoffrey Dawson, the editor of *The Times*, who suggested to Baldwin on 10 September that the National Government should fight the election itself.[15] Baldwin was receptive, and within a few days the Conservative leadership was pressing hard for the idea. For different reasons, however, MacDonald and the Liberals were much less receptive. Lloyd George, still the titular leader of the Liberal Party, had more to lose from an election than any other leading politician. An untimely prostate operation had kept him out of action throughout the crisis, and he was still recovering at Churt. If the government stayed in office, he could look forward to taking part in it before long. In an early election, he would be consigned to the margin of events. Not surprisingly, Lloyd George was vehemently opposed to Dawson's solution, and did all he could to frustrate it. Samuel, and the section of the Liberal Party for which Samuel spoke, were only one degree less opposed. They were as committed to free trade as the Conservatives were to protection, and they could see as easily as the Conservatives could that an early election would probably produce a protectionist majority. MacDonald was not as opposed as the Liberals, but he was profoundly unenthusiastic. He was still a member of the

Labour Party, and in spite of his growing contempt for its new leadership, he still felt the pull of old loyalties and friendships. It is possible that he still hoped to return to it when the crisis was over. It is certain that the thought of leading Conservatives and Liberals into an election campaign against it was deeply distasteful to him.

For a while, he prevaricated – giving Dawson the impression that he would be willing to fight an election, but warning the King that if he did so his position would be 'very anomalous':[16] chairing a long Cabinet discussion on the nature of a possible National Government appeal, but warning Baldwin and Samuel that, although an election might be 'good political tactics', it would 'produce [a] financial crisis.'[17] But he was not able to prevaricate for long. The drain of sterling accelerated after the so-called Invergordon mutiny on 15 September, and on 18 September the Cabinet decided to leave the gold standard after all. This destroyed the strongest argument against an election, for there was no need to avoid a financial crisis which had already happened. It also strengthened the Conservatives' bargaining position. Hitherto, they had been locked into the Government by the logic which had led them to join it in the first place. Having agreed to serve under MacDonald on the grounds that only a National Government could save the country from a forced devaluation, they were bound in honour to go on serving under him until the danger of a forced devaluation disappeared. Now that devaluation had come and gone, the lock was broken. The Conservatives still believed that it was in the national interest for the government to survive; with good reason, they also believed that it was in their party interests. But if they were forced to choose between its survival and an election, they were now free to choose the latter. In the ten days following the decision to leave the gold standard, the Conservative pressure for an election became steadily more clamorous and more difficult to resist.

By a curious, but perhaps appropriate, irony, however, the decisive twist of the screw came from the Labour Party. By mid-September, a number of Labour backbenchers had discovered that there was more sympathy for MacDonald among ordinary party members than they had expected; one of them told Herbert Usher, MacDonald's political secretary, that in his constituency 'whole blocks of people' were refusing to pay their subscriptions because they did not understand why the party had treated MacDonald so badly.[18] Meanwhile, Henderson's leadership had come under fire from the Left, and there were rumours that he might be prepared to come to terms with MacDonald, either by joining a reconstituted National Government, or by helping MacDonald to return to the Labour Party.[19] These rumours were, no doubt, exaggerated, but it is unlikely that they had no foundation at all. It is even less likely that they were unknown to the extra-parliamentary leadership, which had been in effective control of the Labour Party since the fall of the Labour Government, and to which a *rapprochement* between MacDonald and Henderson would have been a serious threat. Perhaps to ensure that no such *rapprochement* took place, perhaps only out of a muddled sense that it was the logical thing to do, the Labour Party executive decided on 28 September – Henderson significantly dissenting – that all members and supporters of the National Government should 'automatically and immediately' cease to be members of the Labour Party. Though MacDonald had written a Cabinet paper two days before, arguing that an election was now inevitable, he had not yet burned his boats; on the day the Labour Party Executive took its decision, Clive Wigram reported to the King that MacDonald did not want an election and had 'hopes of sitting tight now and attracting a following of [*sic*] the Labour Party'.[20] The National Executive made nonsense of such hopes, and dealt MacDonald a wounding emotional blow in the process. It also dealt a wounding blow to the Labour movement. The chief barrier to an election has been MacDonald's reluctance to campaign against the Labour Party. On 28 September that barrier was removed.

It was not until a week later, however, that the decision to hold an election was finally taken, and the negotiations that preceded it showed that the balance of forces in the Cabinet was still much more even than an outside observer would have been likely to guess. For the Conservatives, the chief point of an election was to produce a protectionist majority; though they had been converted to the notion of a National Government election, they took it for granted that the Government would fight the kind of campaign which Baldwin had promised them at the end of August – 'a straight fight on tariffs and against the Socialist party'. Precisely because such a campaign was so clearly in the Conservatives' interests, it was out of the question for MacDonald. For the Samuelite Liberal made it clear at an early stage in the proceedings that if the government fought on a protectionist platform, it would do so without them. A Samuelite secession held no terrors for the Conservatives. The right wing of the Liberal Party, led by Sir John Simon, had come out in favour of protection, and the Conservatives were eager to drive Samuel out of the government so that Simon could replace him. For MacDonald, however, Samuel's presence in the government was a political, and indeed an emotional, necessity. He had staked his reputation on the proposition that the National Government would not be a Conservative government in disguise. If the Samuelites left, that proposition would be untenable. It was therefore essential for him that the government should not wage a 'straight fight on tariffs'; and, after a long and complex struggle, he prevailed. On 5 October, the Cabinet at last decided that parliament should be dissolved on the 7th. It also decided that the government as such should say nothing about tariffs one way or the other, but that its constituent parties should be left 'to deal with the question of restriction of imports . . . each in its own way'.[21]

The first National Government, whose life ended, for all practical purposes, with the decision to hold an election, was a temporary expedient, but a surprisingly well-balanced one. The second National Government, which was formed after the votes were counted, was hopelessly unbalanced; and largely for that reason the air of permanence which it wore at the outset rapidly disappeared. It had 556 supporters in the House of Commons, against the official Labour Party's 46; its majority over all parties was 500. But 471 of its supporters were Conservatives; and although MacDonald was obsessively anxious not to allow himself to appear as a 'Tory tool', the weight of numbers was too much for him. Initially, at least, his personal authority stood high. The election had been fought largely on his actions in August, and the results showed that he was supported by an overwhelming majority of the electorate: morally at least, the Government's majority was his as much as the Conservatives'. But this was inevitably a waning asset: the massive Conservative presence in the House of Commons was a permanent one. It was also a visible one, and in some ways this was even more disturbing to their allies. Before the election, charges of Conservative domination could be rebutted by pointing to the fact that the Conservatives had no independent majority in the House of Commons, and therefore needed their allies almost as much as their allies needed them. Now they were perfectly capable of forming a government on their own, and everyone knew it. The result was a strange air of tension, which hung over the government until its break-up ten months later. For the Samuelite Liberals were even more anxious than MacDonald to show that they had not been captured by the Conservatives, and the size of the Conservative majority made it necessary for them to bend over backwards to do so. That, in turn, made it necessary for the Conservatives to prove that Conservative principles were not being watered down. and once principle reared its head, compromise became impossible.

Once again. the Conservatives were given a much smaller share of ministerial posts than they were entitled to by the arithmetic of the House of Commons. More than 80 per cent of the Government backbenchers were Conservatives, but in the Cabinet they had only 11 places out of 20. MacDonald's tiny National Labour group, with only 13 M.P.s to its credit, had four places in the Cabinet. The Samuelite Liberals, with 33 M.P.s, had three and the Simonites, with 35 M.P.s, had two. On policy questions, too, the non-Conservative members of the Cabinet had more influence than has sometimes been realised. Foreign policy, which became increasingly important after the opening of the Disarmament Conference in February 1932, was effectively controlled by MacDonald, with intermittent assistance from Simon, the

Foreign Secretary; in spite of an occasional foray by Baldwin, the Conservatives had little influence on it. On India, MacDonald and his National Labour Lord Chancellor, Sankey, won some modest victories against Conservative opposition. On the central question of fiscal policy, however, the Conservatives were determined to have their way, and their determination carried all before it.

The process began five days after the Cabinet appointments were announced, when Chamberlain, the Chancellor of the Exchequer, warned his colleagues that the already unhealthy trade balance was rapidly deteriorating and that something would have to be done immediately to cut down the flow of imports. The result was the Abnormal Importations Act, which was passed a few days later and which gave the Board of Trade power to impose duties of up to 100 per cent on a wide range of goods. But although the free traders were prepared to accept temporary import restrictions, to deal with a situation which was acknowledged to be abnormal, they were not prepared to abandon the free-trade faith which they had preached all their lives. For the Conservatives, however, temporary restrictions to deal with an abnormal situation were not enough: they wanted full-blooded protection, without apologies or excuses. MacDonald did his best to discover common ground on which both sides could stand without humiliation, but his attempts to do so were ignored. At the beginning of December, he circulated a paper to the Cabinet, arguing that the fiscal question should be seen as a practical rather than as a theoretical one, which should be settled by examining the facts rather than by appealing to doctrine. Neither side took any notice. Instead, the Conservatives insisted, on *a priori* grounds, that the trade balance could be put right only by a generalised tariff, while the free traders replied by rehearsing the classical free-trade dogmas. In the end, the Cabinet did find a compromise of sorts. It was agreed that the generalised tariff should be introduced, but it was also agreed that the free-trade ministers should be allowed to speak and vote against it. But the notorious 'agreement to differ' only patched the government up; it did not restore it to health. The Samuelites, accompanied by the bleak and solitary figure of Philip Snowden, finally left the government in September 1932 in protest against the Ottawa agreements. In spirit, they had left nine months before.

MacDonald and the rest of the National Labour group stayed on; so did the Simonites. But although ministers still insisted on wearing their National labels, and although MacDonald made repeated attempts to convince himself and others that he still headed a non-party government, these attempts were so unconvincing that the story can reasonably be considered to have ended here. Even now, MacDonald was more than the helpless figurehead which he has sometimes been depicted as being. In spite of failing health, declining powers and

growing personal unhappiness, he had more influence on the government's foreign policy than any other single member of it, at any rate
until the end of 1933 and perhaps until the summer of 1934. Though his
occasional attempts to influence its financial and economic policies
were usually beaten off without much difficulty, he was not the only
prime minister of whom that could be said. But such influence as he
possessed came partly from his personal grasp of the issues involved – in
discussions on foreign affairs, as Lord Avon put it later, he displayed
the 'touch of the master'[22] – and partly from his office. It did not come
from the support of a party. The same was true of the other non-Conservative ministers. Some had influence and others did not. But when
they had it, it came from the persuasiveness of their arguments and the
weight of their departments in the Whitehall scales, not from the
presence of organised parties at their backs. The Samuelite Liberals
were, no doubt, a weak party, with little popular support and few
distinctive policies. But they were nevertheless a recognisable party,
with a tradition, a sense of identity and organised loyalties across the
country. None of this was true of the National Liberals or of
MacDonald's National Labour followers. Before the free traders left,
the government had been a genuine coalition, albeit an extremely
lopsided one. Now it was a Conservative government, headed by a non-
Conservative, and with a number of other non-Conservatives dotted
uneasily about.

What went wrong? Only a year before, the electorate had given what
it believed to be a non-party government the most crushing parliamentary majority of modern times. Why did that government turn so
rapidly into a party government? Why, having received the 'doctor's
mandate', did the physician demonstrate such a marked incapacity for
self-cure? One possible answer – the answer which the free traders gave
at the time and which a number of historians have echoed since – is that
it was all the fault of the Conservatives. 'The country had put the
various Parties in office together in order to adopt an agreed policy
...', Samuel complained at his last Cabinet meeting, 'but on fiscal
matters there had been no common policy. All the sacrifices had come
from the Free Traders'.[23] The Conservatives, Snowden wrote, in an
anguished letter to MacDonald just before his resignation, 'have sacrificed nothing, but have used the enormous Tory majority we gave them
at the Election to carry out a Tory policy and to identify us with it'.[24]
That answer undoubtedly contains an element of truth. There is no way
of knowing how many Conservative M.P.s had been returned to
Westminster only because normally Liberal or Labour voters had voted
the National ticket, but there must have been a significant number.
Having won their majority, moreover, the Conservatives rapidly made
it clear that they were determined to have protection at the earliest
possible moment, and that, if necessary, they were prepared to bring the

government down in order to get it. Yet it is hard to see what else they could have been expected to do. Neither side showed any willingness to compromise: if the sacrifices had not come from the free traders, they would have had to come from the protectionists. Since the protectionists believed protection to be indispensible, said so to the electorate and won a huge majority after having said so, they could be forgiven for thinking that no sacrifices should come from them. Implicit in Samuel's complaint was the unspoken assumption that, whereas the free traders had a right to believe in free trade, the protectionists did not have a right to believe in protection. That was not an assumption which the protectionists could be expected to share.

The true answer lies deeper. Coalitions last only as long as the parties composing them believe that the survival of the coalition is more important than the uninhibited pursuit of their party interests. That was true of the coalitions in both world wars, and it was true of Lloyd George's peacetime coalition until the eve of its collapse. It was true of the National Government only for a brief period at the end of August and the beginning of September 1931. During that period, all the constituent parties showed a remarkable willingness to compromise, because they all believed that it would be a disaster for the country if the government fell. Once the gold standard was abandoned, they ceased to believe it. Before the election, the Conservatives still wanted MacDonald and were prepared to make concessions to keep him: that was why they agreed to the 'doctor's mandate', and stopped insisting that the whole government should fight on a protectionist platform. After the election, they still regarded MacDonald's presence in the government as an asset, but they did not regard it as an asset for which it was worth paying a high price. The free traders' presence they did not even regard as an asset: if anything, they saw it as a liability. If they could have got rid of the free traders before the election without losing MacDonald in the process, they would have been happy to do so. When the free traders departed in the end, their reaction was one of relief rather than disappointment. But all this was as true of the Liberals as it was of the Conservatives. Samuel and his followers could, after all, have resigned from the government before the election, and fought as an independent party in the way that Lloyd George wanted them to. The reason they did not do so was that they correctly believed that they would lose heavily if they did. What they wanted was to fight under the National banner, without giving up their distinctive position; thanks to MacDonald, that was what they managed to do. Their behaviour after the election was equally calculated. They stayed in the government as long as they believed that it was in their party interests to do so, and left when they came to the conclusion that it was no longer in their party interests. Their calculations, moreover, were much better judged than the Conservatives. By staying in the government in October 1931 they ensured their survival as a significant parliamentary force; by leaving it in September 1932 they ensured their continued existence as a separate party. Samuel does not have a high place in the pantheon of Liberal leaders. But if he had not displayed great skill in playing a weak hand between September 1931 and September 1932, it is doubtful if the Liberal Party would exist today.

# 4 1932–1945

## A. J. P. TAYLOR

The government that Winston Churchill formed on 10 May 1940 was
more than a coalition. It was the only genuine National government in
British history. The term 'National' implies national unity and a
readiness to put country before party. No other government has had
these characteristics to the full. Previous coalitions, with perhaps the
exception of Asquith's from 1915 to 1916, were always faced with
avowed opposition benches, and the supporters of coalition by no
means neglected party considerations. Churchill's government was in
the unique position of commanding the almost unanimous allegiance of
both parliament and country.

The three principal political parties adhered to it by formal decisions;
dissent came only from the minuscule Independent Labour Party of
three and the solitary Communist, who relinquished his dissent after 22
July 1941. There was sometimes inter-party dispute over individual
topics; there was sometimes discontent in the country over wartime
conditions. But the existence of the National government was rarely
threatened and Churchill, its Prime Minister, maintained an
unparalleled, though occasionally fluctuating, prestige throughout the
war.[1]

Such an achievement might have been expected to have been long a-
growing with national unity gradually becoming a habit. Quite the
contrary was the case. The decade of the 1930s was marked by bitter
party conflict and deep resentments. The so-called National Government had won an overwhelming majority at the general election of 1931
and a great, though lesser, majority at that of 1935; its preponderance
was little shaken by the secession of some thirty Liberals under Sir
Herbert Samuel in 1932. But the Labour party continued to exist,
however diminished – a mere fifty M.P.s in 1931 and some hundred and
fifty in 1935; and it was a party of sharp opposition. For Labour the
National Government was from the first a fraud and a cheat, and its
very name made the idea of national unity abhorrent to Labour
supporters.

Though Labour's resentment was at first directed against Ramsay
MacDonald, the leader who had supposedly betrayed his party, it was
more significant that the principal exponent of the National
Government's economic policy was Neville Chamberlain, then

Chancellor of the Exchequer and the very man who was prime minister of the so-called National Government when war broke out in 1939. Chamberlain came to personify in Labour eyes all the evils that the so-called National Government stood for. He reciprocated Labour's hostility. As Attlee, Labour's leader after 1935, said: 'He always treated us like dirt.'

The supporters of the National Government claimed to monopolise national unity and Labour was written off as the unpatriotic party. There was class war in social relations. Few Labour men belonged to the West End clubs and Hugh Dalton, Eton and King's, was regarded with peculiar hostility as a traitor to his class. There were none of the private friendships between antagonists that there had been, say, between Churchill and F. E. Smith before 1914 or between Baldwin and MacDonald in the 1920s. In 1913 Bonar Law, the Unionist leader, was invited to Balmoral at the height of the Ulster conflict. Neither Lansbury nor Attlee, the two Labour leaders, was ever invited to Buckingham Palace, let alone Balmoral. Balfour had known all the secrets of defence in the days of the Asquith government. Baldwin and MacDonald exchanged these secrets whichever of them was in office. No Labour man learnt anything of defence problems in the 1930s until shortly before the outbreak of war.

The bitterness was at first greatest over economic affairs, with two million unemployed and the hunger marchers at the door. The estrangement grew deeper when foreign affairs took first place. Both government and opposition were in confusion. The National Government was accused of surrendering to the aggressive powers over Manchuria, Abyssinia and central Europe. Labour was accused of advocating strong measures and disarmament at the same time. But how could Labour place arms in the hands of ministers who, they feared, would not use them against the aggressors and might well use them against Soviet Russia? The Spanish civil war carried this estrangement to its highest point. The Labour party championed the Spanish Republic. The government acquiesced in the victory of Spanish Fascism and perhaps even welcomed it. Labour was accused of being in alliance with the Communists; the National Government of betraying national interests because of its Fascist predilections.

Straddling the two contenders there were non-party intellectuals, fertile in ideas though with no voting strength. Most of these men preferred the National Government to Labour, but they tried to offer alternative policies. In economics they sought 'a middle way', equally remote from socialism and *laissez-faire*. Similarly, collective security was by no means a cause confined to the Labour Party. Indeed the so-called Peace Ballot, actually a great demonstration in favour of collective security, was initiated and conducted by the LNU, not the Labour Party, and owed its success mainly to middle-class support.

These enlightened 'do-gooders' rarely carried their differences with the National Government to the point of voting against it. In 1935 there was an indignant outcry against the Hoare–Laval plan in which many Conservative M.P.s joined, but only two of them – Vyvyan Adams and Harold Macmillan – voted against the final abandonment of Abyssinia, and this was the only occasion when any National supporters went openly against the government. Some 30 Conservatives abstained from voting at the time of Eden's resignation; some 40 abstained after Munich. None voted against the government. Eden and his small group did not regard themselves as in opposition and kept clear of Churchill as too provocative a figure. Even Churchill never called for the defeat of the National Government, despite his sharp criticism of its policy, and never yet received'. On 10 June, after the British withdrawal from Crete, there was another debate, though this time no division.
his mind.

Throughout the 1930s there were also repeated attempts, again more talk than action, to find a true national leader in place of MacDonald, Baldwin or Chamberlain. Lloyd George was at first the favoured candidate. After all he had headed a national coalition and was the man who had won the war. He was now isolated, with no supporters in parliament except members of his own family; perhaps this was itself a recommendation. Advocacy of Lloyd George grew so strong that in 1935 he was almost invited to join the National Government – almost but not quite. Thereafter he became only the shadow of a great name.

Sir Stafford Cripps was also a possible, though self-nominated saviour of the country. At one time he advocated a United Front of the three Left-wing socialist groups – his own Socialist League, the ILP and the Communist Party. Later he switched to a Popular Front of Labour, Liberals and dissident Conservatives, a tactic that actually produced an electoral victory at Bridgwater. The Popular Front encountered implacable hostility from Labour leaders, who held that voting Labour was the only alternative to supporting the National Government. Cripps himself was expelled from the Labour Party in 1939. In his own opinion, though not in that of anyone else, he still remained capable of devising a government of national salvation, if not of leading it.

When all other candidates for national leadership were eliminated, only Churchill was left. He and Lloyd George were the only great figures surviving from the First World War and Churchill, unlike Lloyd George, was still at the height of his powers. His very achievements provoked general, if not universal, distrust. It was an axiom of politics that Labour would never work with him. Labour men had long memories, despite their comparatively recent experiences of politics. They cherished the myth of Tonypandy when Churchill allegedly sent troops into action against miners on strike. They remembered Churchill's leadership in the wars of intervention against Soviet Russia and his conduct of the *British Gazette* during the General Strike. They were not mollified by Churchill's sharp reproaches against Labour's opposition to rearmament.

Labour was not alone in distrust. Churchill was almost equally unpopular in the Conservative ranks. Older Conservatives remembered the attacks on landowners by Churchill, grandson of a duke, during his Radical phase before the First World War. Younger, more enlightened, Conservatives were exasperated by the four-year campaign that Churchill had waged against the Government of India Bill. His persistent alarms over German rearmament in time wearied the Commons. Members of all parties were outraged by his chivalrous, though misguided, championing of Edward VIII at the time of the abdication.

Many civil servants shared this distrust. A few, such as Vansittart, secretly co-operated with him. Hankey, the most powerful civil servant of the time, was more representative when he dismissed Churchill as 'a wild elephant'. Above all, Churchill was distrusted by those in the highest political places. Baldwin might say, 'We must keep Churchill in reserve as Prime Minister in case there is a great war', but perhaps this was a tactful way of keeping him out of office. Neville Chamberlain, who became prime minister in 1937, had no such reservations. He had been a colleague of Churchill's in the Conservative government of 1924–9 and had bitter memories of that time. When they were supposed to be working together on an ambitious scheme for derating, he had found Churchill ill-informed, egocentric and disloyal. Again and again Churchill would steal the limelight, usually with half-baked proposals. Often Chamberlain reached the point of declaring that he could go on no longer. In the end he reluctantly acquiesced but he was determined never to have Churchill as a colleague again.

Chamberlain's hostility towards Churchill was seconded by Sir Samuel Hoare, one of Chamberlain's closest associates. He, too, had bitter memories, in his case over Churchill's opposition to the Government of India Bill. It seemed to him that Churchill had been ruthless, unscrupulous and impervious to argument. He, too, was determined never to co-operate with Churchill again. Of the other leading ministers Sir John Simon had no reason to love Churchill, and Halifax, though more easy-going, felt little inclination to support him. Some junior ministers hankered after Churchill but in Chamberlain's system of government they carried no weight. Broadly, exclusion of Churchill was one of the few questions on which National Government and its supporters were united.

At times Churchill seemed on the point of a breakthrough. His advocacy of collective security in 1936 won him wide support. But as so often he threw it away, first by his favourable attitude to Franco at the beginning of the Spanish civil war and then by his defence of Edward

VIII. Each time Churchill climbed up a ladder only to land on a snake and slip down again. He was not blind to his reputation for irresponsibility. As he said later, 'Remember, I have the medals of Antwerp, Gallipoli, Norway and elsewhere pinned to my chest.' After the Munich crisis he was attacked in his own constituency association and, despairing of his future, proposed to withdraw from public life. He remained 'a busted flush', in Beaverbrook's phrase, almost until the moment of his triumph.

Hence Neville Chamberlain reigned supreme despite much criticism and many failures. He was in no need of a National Government. He believed he had one already. Those who supported him composed the Nation. All others including Conservatives who criticised him, such as Churchill and to a lesser extent Eden, were beyond the pale. This outlook was shared by most of his supporters. Though Chamberlain was efficient, clear-headed and a redoubtable debater, he appears in retrospect singularly unlovable. This was not how he appeared at the time. No Conservative leader has commanded greater loyalty and even affection, feelings that withstood repeated setbacks. Attacks on Chamberlain merely strengthened the devotion of his followers and increased party antagonisms. The divisions which had characterised British political life since 1931 did not diminish as war approached. Rather they grew deeper. Chamberlain did not regret this. Intellectually contemptuous of his critics, he had no wish to recruit them for his government. After Munich, Halifax advised Chamberlain to bring in Churchill and Eden. Chamberlain took no notice. Even after the British guarantee to Poland made war likely, he was more concerned to ward off a Soviet alliance than to win over his critics. At the outbreak of war Chamberlain's supporters in the Commons numbered 418; Labour numbered 167; Labour and Liberals together did not total 200. Why should Chamberlain with a majority of well over 200 worry over these barking dogs? Like the proverbial caravan he passed on, confident in his own wisdom and power.

On 1 September, the Germans invaded Poland. There was no answering declaration of war by Great Britain. On 2 September, Chamberlain and Halifax were still marking time. It was claimed later that the hesitations came from the French. It seemed at the time – and in my opinion this is the more likely explanation – that Chamberlain and Halifax were still hoping for some German withdrawal or the proposal of a conference by Mussolini. When that evening Chamberlain still spoke in terms of delay, there was general unrest in the House with simple-minded Conservatives the most restive. As Arthur Greenwood, deputising for Attlee, rose to speak, there was a cry from Amery on the Conservative benches, 'Speak for England, Arthur!' Greenwood did his best and called for a declaration of war. Even Chamberlain's most loyal followers deserted him. Margesson, the Conservative chief whip, said that there would be no holding the House next day unless war was declared. None other than Sir John Simon carried a message to Chamberlain from eleven Cabinet ministers that war must be declared at once. Chamberlain acquiesced. War against Germany was declared the next morning. But Amery's cry to Greenwood left its mark. At the critical moment Labour had taken the path of honour. The past was forgotten and the war became implicitly Labour's war. This was the first nail in Chamberlain's coffin.

Chamberlain went through the motions of seeking national unity. On 1 September he condescendingly invited the Labour party to join his government. Labour unhesitatingly refused. They could not, they said, enter a Cabinet led by Chamberlain and Sir John Simon.[2] The Liberals were also offered posts, though not in the War Cabinet. They, too, refused. Chamberlain made one concession. He brought Eden and Churchill back into the government, a concession that was little more than window-dressing. Eden, at the Dominions Office, was outside the War Cabinet and contributed little. Churchill, as First Lord of the Admiralty and with a seat in the War Cabinet, was a more formidable figure. But he still stood much alone, safely penned in, it seemed, by ministers and civil servants loyal to Chamberlain.

Ostensibly party warfare was laid aside. On 8 September the three chief whips, following the precedent of the First World War, agreed to an electoral truce for the duration: when a vacancy occurred, the party which had previously held the seat would nominate a candidate unopposed by the other two parties. The new functions of the Ministry of Information also stimulated co-operation between the parties. In the first war the ministry had concerned itself solely with propaganda abroad; this time its activities were directed towards public opinion at home, and representatives of the three parties met on its local committees. In practice the Ministry of Information was more concerned to keep the public quiet than to arouse patriotic enthusiasm. The groundswell of public opinion, if it existed, has to be sought in more obscure places elsewhere.

Here is a central problem of our theme and one that can never be solved with certainty. Between September 1939 and May 1940 Churchill greatly enhanced his reputation and many people came to regard him as the national leader, almost without knowing that they were doing so. But there is no sure way of describing how this came about. Churchill himself contributed much. This was not by deliberate purpose: he truly meant to be a loyal colleague, above all not to go into the wilderness again. But, being Churchill, he could not help being exuberant and advertising himself with every speech, almost with every gesture. He was the only colourful figure in the government, the only one who stood out as a man. His speeches breathed the spirit of total war when Chamberlain was still hoping for a compromise peace. In the period of the phoney war, with no fighting on land and virtually no activity in the air, the deeds of the navy provided the only news and the only drama. Such events as the destruction of the *Graf Spee* and the liberation of the British prisoners on the *Altmark* redounded to Churchill's credit; they were what the war was really about.

The real struggle for power went on behind the scenes, with Churchill once more going into battle almost unintentionally. The fundamental question of the first war was: who should direct the war? Lloyd George thrust the question on Asquith when he proposed a War Committee of three with himself in the chair. Asquith believed that this would reduce his own position as prime minister to a cipher. He therefore rejected Lloyd George's proposal. In the ensuing conflict he was brought down and Lloyd George was raised up.

Ostensibly Chamberlain followed the Lloyd George precedent when he established a War Cabinet on the outbreak of war. His first intention, it seems, was to give Churchill direction of the war by making him a member of the War Cabinet without a department to administer. On second thoughts he assigned the Admiralty to Churchill and on third thoughts weakened Churchill's position still further by bringing the two other service ministers – the Secretary for War and the Secretary for Air – into the War Cabinet also. As well, Chatfield, the Minister for Co-ordination of Defence, was included in the War Cabinet, reporting to it the views of the chiefs of staff – a nonsensical arrangement when the three service ministers were now in the War Cabinet and could do it themselves. The purpose of this clumsy system, so far as it had one, was to bar the way against Churchill's direction of the war. In the tangle of authorities Chamberlain, as prime minister, was still supreme.

This was the theory. The practice was different. Whenever Churchill was a member of a Cabinet there was no holding him. Not content to run his own department flamboyantly, he intervened in the running of every other. He had done this in Lloyd George's post-war Cabinet, conducting his own foreign policy without regard for Curzon, the Foreign Secretary, and pronouncing on every topic from economics to Ireland, until Lloyd George came to wonder who was prime minister – Churchill or himself. So now Churchill, once established at the Admiralty, behaved quite without intention as though he were already prime minister. He directed a stream of letters to Chamberlain on the conduct of the war. Chamberlain expostulated that this was unnecessary when they met every day in Cabinet. Churchill was contrite but the letters were soon resumed. Churchill accompanied Chamberlain to meetings of the Allied Supreme Council and took the lead in the discussions of strategy. He made public statements on foreign policy, quite contrary to the views of Lord Halifax. He inquired into economic policy and labour relations. This inexhaustible display of energy exasperated some of his colleagues, and many civil servants even more so.

Chamberlain himself was exasperated. Yet strangely enough he gradually gave way, almost as though he recognised that Churchill could conduct the war and he himself could not. Or perhaps, as troubles mounted, he planned to make Churchill the scapegoat or 'an air raid shelter to keep the splinters from hitting his colleagues', in Lloyd George's wounding phrase. Whatever the explanation, Chamberlain did little to resist Churchill's encroachments despite complaints from other ministers.

The first open shift of power came at the beginning of April 1940 when Chatfield finally wearied of his empty role as Minister for the Co-ordination of Defence and resigned. Chamberlain appointed no successor to Chatfield. Instead he asked Churchill to preside over the military co-ordination committee which consisted of the three service ministers and the three chiefs of staff. Churchill was delighted, the more so when real war began with the German invasion of Norway on 8 April. Of course Churchill was not content to preside. He already behaved as Minister of Defence, bullying the chiefs of staff and presenting the committee with decisions which he had forced on the chiefs of staff beforehand. On 16 April the other two service ministers revolted and appealed to Chamberlain, who agreed to take the chair at the committee himself. A week later Churchill revolted in the opposite direction and demanded that Chamberlain appoint a deputy to 'concert and direct the general movement of our war action'. Chamberlain yielded and, when the other two service ministers threatened to resign, answered that in that case he would resign himself. Thus Churchill had won the same battle against Chamberlain that Lloyd George had lost against Asquith in 1916. According to Sir John Reith, Chamberlain also said that if Churchill were to be debunked he was not the man to do it. But Reith was not a very reliable witness.

These changes were not appreciated outside the Cabinet. What the public and the backbenchers saw was the failure in Norway. Here little groups of the discontented which had sprung up since the outbreak of war perhaps came into their own. Clement Davies, a one-time Liberal National, presided over an All-Party Action Group which in fact provided more talk than action. So far as it had a programme, it was to promote the fortunes of Lloyd George. Later Lord Salisbury set up a Watching Committee of critical Conservatives on the analogy of the Unionist Business Committee during the First World War. So far this committee had done nothing except watch. When Clement Davies told Attlee about these two groups, Attlee replied that nothing could be done until Conservatives came out openly against Chamberlain. This was also the opinion of Beaverbrook, an expert in the making and unmaking of coalitions. Drawing on his experiences during the First World War, he wrote on 7 May: 'In every case the revolt that broke the Government came from within. The same applies this time. Those who try to do it from without are simply wasting their ammunition.'

British forces withdrew from central Norway. In parliament the Whitsun recess was approaching, and the adjournment motion gave opportunity for a two-day debate on 7 and 8 May. Though much criticism was certain, the government was expected to survive. Beaverbrook wrote on 6 May: 'I don't think Chamberlain will be turned out this time. But he remains in office with such an immense volume of disapproval in his own Party, that he had better retire.' Even after the debate, with its disastrous result for Chamberlain, early editions of *The Times* and the *Manchester Guardian* appeared with leaders lamenting Labour's decision to force a division because it would only solidify the government ranks. This was exactly what the Labour leaders feared and their first decision was against a division. So reluctantly did they go into battle.

The sensation of the first day's debate on 7 May was Amery's speech with its peroration, repeating Cromwell's words to the Long Parliament, 'You have sat too long for any good you have been doing. Depart, I say, and let us have done with you. In the name of God, go.' Even then the All-Party Group and other rebellious Conservatives 'on the whole inclined to deprecate a division'. Similarly Lord Salisbury and his Watching Committee strongly advised Conservative M.P.s not to vote against the government. Decision rested with Labour's Parliamentary Executive Committee. Afterwards many claimed the honour of taking the lead. In 1954 Attlee said that it was he who recommended a division. In 1960 Morrison said that all the Labour leaders were shocked when he proposed to divide the house. Dalton recorded in his diary that the majority of the Executive was for a division, though he himself was against. At the meeting of the Parliamentary Labour Party the proposal for a division was opposed by the spokesmen of the Left, Aneurin Bevan and George Strauss, again because it would only strengthen Chamberlain.

It is impossible to determine what really happened. Probably most Labour leaders trembled at the thought of a division and finally could not shrink from one. I add one explanation which derives only from a conversation with Lady Astor – another unreliable witness. According to her the women M.P.s, who met in an all-party room of their own, resolved to force a vote if no one else did so. Mavis Tate, a Conservative M.P., was strongest for this course. Ellen Wilkinson, a Labour M.P. and a very close friend of Morrison's, took the news to him. If this story is true, Morrison had good reason to advocate a decision rather than have one thrust on him by the women. At all events Lady Astor voted against the government when the time came.

When the House met on 8 May Morrison announced that Labour would call for a division. Chamberlain appealed to 'his friends – and I have friends in the House'. Lloyd George, in his last great speech, told Chamberlain to make an example of sacrifice 'because there is nothing which can contribute more to victory in this war than that he should sacrifice the seals of office'. Churchill made the best case he could for the government. At a private conclave the All-Party group and others decided to vote against Chamberlain. At the division 41 of those who usually supported the government voted with the opposition and some 80 more did not vote. The government's majority fell from about 220 to 81 (281 for, 200 against). Not all the abstentions were deliberate gestures of no confidence. 15 were paired and some 30 more later claimed that they had been unavoidably absent. Against this some Conservatives later alleged that they had voted for the government only because of a promise from Margesson, the Conservative chief whip, that the government would be reconstructed afterwards. In any case what the public and M.P.s saw at the time was the figure of 80 abstentions and did not enquire how these had come about.

Clement Davies took the credit for bringing out the anti-Chamberlain vote and established a reputation as the author of Chamberlain's fall. This is an exaggeration. The All-Party Action Group may have started the rush by swinging some ten or twelve votes. But another ten came from discontented serving officers and the rest from M.P.s who had not gone against Chamberlain previously. The vote was mainly a spontaneous revolt, perhaps helped by conversations in the smoking-room and by messages from the constituencies. However this may be, the House of Commons showed its power in a way unprecedented in the First World War.

Chamberlain was still prime minister with presumably a rock-hard majority of 81. But his self-confidence had been gravely shaken and he recognised that he would have to reconstruct his government. His first thought the next morning was to offer posts to Amery and other Conservative rebels. The rebels stopped this move by a public statement that they would support any prime minister who enjoyed the confidence of the country and could form a national government – a polite way of saying that Labour must be included. Curiously enough this seemed to work against Churchill, who was still distrusted by the Labour party. Lord Halifax made a brief appearance as a possible prime minister. Attlee, Morrison and Dalton wanted Halifax. So did Cripps, Lloyd George and Sir Archibald Sinclair. George VI also preferred Halifax, though he did not make this known until too late.

Churchill on his side still distrusted Labour and believed that they had nothing to contribute. Cautious to the last he declared that he would serve with or under anyone. Attempts were made to shake this high-minded resolve. Beaverbrook tried in vain. Bracken, Churchill's acolyte, was more successful. He reported that Attlee, though preferring Halifax, would not refuse to serve under Churchill. Bracken urged that Churchill, if asked to serve under Halifax, should make no reply.[3] It is by no means certain that this conversation ever took place, though the story of it was widely known within a few days.

The actual course of events was less dramatic. On the afternoon of

9 May Chamberlain summoned Churchill, Halifax and Margesson, the Conservative chief whip, to 10 Downing Street. He asked what should he report to the King? Margesson answered that the Conservatives could no longer be relied on to support him and that he should resign. In answer to a further question Margesson said that the House of Commons (or according to another version 'some Conservatives') would prefer Halifax as prime minister. There was a long pause. To Churchill it seemed longer than the two minutes' silence on Armistice Day. Halifax broke the silence by saying that his peerage would make it impossible for him to carry out the function of prime minister. His private reasons were that the very thought of becoming prime minister gave him a bad pain in the stomach and that, whoever was prime minister, Churchill would run the show.

No more was said.[4] Churchill and Halifax went out to have tea in the garden. Chamberlain meanwhile received Attlee and Greenwood and invited them to join his government. They declined to answer until they had consulted the National Executive Committee of the Labour Party at Bournemouth where the party was assembling for its annual conference, but they expected the answer would be 'No'. Chamberlain grudgingly asked whether Labour would be prepared to serve under someone else. Here the answer was left open.

During the night of 9–10 May the Germans invaded Holland and Belgium. Chamberlain thought this was no time to rock the boat. He appeared at the Cabinet 'in good form; the news from the Low Countries had stimulated him ... He was ready for action if encouraged and authorised to act.' Kingsley Wood cut in that now more than ever Chamberlain must go. In the afternoon Labour's answer came from Bournemouth: Labour would 'take its full and equal share as full partner in a new Government under a new Prime Minister which would command the confidence of the nation'. Chamberlain recognised that the end had come.

Within an hour Chamberlain went to Buckingham Palace and resigned as prime minister. The King, after expressing his own preference for Halifax, asked Chamberlain to recommend his successor. Chamberlain answered 'that H. was not enthusiastic' and the King agreed that it must be Churchill. At six o'clock in the evening Churchill became prime minister. There was thus technically no upheaval, no interregnum as there had been in 1916 and again in 1931, when one prime minister had resigned and another had not been found to take his place. In constitutional parlance Chamberlain merely resigned and after doing so formally named his successor. Many men claimed the credit for making Churchill prime minister. Clement Davies claimed it; Bracken claimed it; the Conservative rebels claimed it; Kingsley Wood claimed it; Labour claimed it. In cold fact it was Chamberlain who made Churchill prime minister, as he had probably intended to do all along. Maybe he kept Halifax in reserve to make peace if things were wrong; all the same Churchill as prime minister was Chamberlain's creation.

Unlike Lloyd George in the first war, Churchill meant to work with parliament and the three political parties, not to break free of them. His National Government, as Lloyd George complained, was 'a Coalition of Parties and their nominees . . . not a War Directorate in the real sense of the term.' Churchill chose most of the principal ministers himself, assisted by Bracken, his confidential adviser.[5] Some of the appointments, such as that of Bevin, were a surprise to the party leader concerned. The junior ministers were nominated by Margesson for the Conservatives and by Attlee, who always took an interest in such things, for Labour.

The party balance was carefully observed for the highest posts. The new War Cabinet was simply an assembly of the party leaders with Churchill in solitary state as the National leader: Chamberlain, leader of the Conservative party; Halifax, Conservative leader in the Lords; Attlee, leader of the Labour Party; and Greenwood, its deputy leader. Some of the members were certainly not chosen for their ability. It was significant of the party alliance that, apart from Churchill, Attlee was the only man who sat in the War Cabinet from the first day to the last.[6] The parties also took equal shares of the three service ministries: Admiralty, Labour (A. V. Alexander); Air Ministry, Liberal (Sinclair); War Office, Conservative (Eden). In the other posts the Conservatives came off best: they held fifteen offices of Cabinet rank, Labour only four and the Liberals one. This was no doubt a recognition of the relative party strengths but it also sprang from the fact that after nine years in office the Conservatives had more men of experience and proved ability. Labour's share improved during the war as more Labour men had the opportunity to show their talents and the Conservatives slipped down still further when men were enlisted from outside politics even if they called themselves Conservatives.

Churchill settled the most troublesome point at once by making himself Minister of Defence. Perhaps he did not realise the full implications of this immediately but in time he assumed sole direction of the operations of war. At first he deferred to the War Cabinet by presiding over a Defence Committee (Operations), composed of two members of the War Cabinet, the three service ministers and the chiefs of staff. Soon he dealt directly with the Chiefs of Staffs Committee, issuing orders to the armed forces indiscriminately in their name or in his own. The figures tell their own story. The Defence Committee (Operations) held 52 meetings in 1940, ten in 1944 and then only to discuss minor topics. Meanwhile the Chiefs of Staffs Committee held more than 400 meetings each year and 573 in 1942. The three service ministers were also deprived of any say over policy and became merely administrators, so much so that in 1942 Churchill appointed a civil servant, Sir James Grigg, as Secretary of State for War without anyone's noticing the difference.

Churchill proposed to make Chamberlain Leader of the House. Labour objected and Churchill took on the job himself, although Attlee often stood in for him. The Conservative and Labour chief whips set up a joint office under Margesson. The Labour M.P.s still occupied the Opposition benches since there was nowhere else for them to go, and the senior Labour ex-minister (at first Lees-Smith and then Greenwood) performed the duties of Leader of the Opposition. There was no real opposition, certainly not from Labour. On the contrary, with the annual conference still in session at Bournemouth, the Labour leaders got formal approval for joining the government by 2,450,000 votes to 170,000. The electoral truce remained in operation and when parliament became due for dissolution in the autumn of 1940, its life was prolonged by annual Acts until the end of the war.[7]

Party unity was at first by no means wholehearted. Conservatives who had remained loyal to Chamberlain resented his overthrow. When Churchill appeared in the house on 13 May to deliver his 'blood, toil, tears and sweat' speech, Conservatives rose and cheered Chamberlain; cheers for Churchill came only from the Labour benches. This sullen gesture was repeated for some weeks until a journalist, Paul Einzig, warned Chamberlain that it was having a bad effect abroad. A few days later, when Churchill rose to speak Margesson waved his handkerchief towards the Conservative benches and at this signal of command the Conservatives cheered. The story is a little too dramatic to ring true. The occasion was Churchill's announcement of the attack on the French fleet at Mers-el-Kebir and perhaps this was enough in itself to bring up the Conservatives. At any rate 'all joined in solemn stentorian applause' (Churchill).

The War Cabinet itself was also at first not without disagreements. On 27 May Halifax advocated an approach to Hitler through Mussolini and was supported by Chamberlain. Attlee and Greenwood opposed the suggestion indignantly. Churchill evaded a decision. However, he took the precaution the next day of assuring a meeting of ministers of cabinet rank: 'Of course, whatever happens at Dunkirk, we shall fight on.' No approach was made to Mussolini. After the fall of France some members of the Foreign Office, perhaps inspired by Halifax, dropped cautious hints about the possibility of a negotiated peace but victory in the Battle of Britain really settled the issue. Thereafter virtually everyone in the world of politics agreed with Churchill's 'victory at all costs', though there were mutterings about a compromise peace in less official circles.

The careful pattern of party balance in the War Cabinet was gradually eroded. In August 1940 Beaverbrook joined it. Though he was technically a Conservative he certainly did not count as one. He

owed his appointment partly to his achievements as Minister of
Aircraft Production and more to Churchill's favour towards an old
friend who provided him with stimulating company. A larger change
came in the autumn of 1940 when Chamberlain fell ill and died.
Churchill was reluctant to abandon his position as the national leader
above party. Beaverbrook persuaded him that it was dangerous for the
leadership of the Conservative Party to be in the hands of anyone else
and Churchill took it. But he rarely considered Conservative Party
interests except when they coincided with his own. Sir John Anderson,
a former civil servant, succeeded Chamberlain in the War Cabinet and
as Lord President – a weakening of the party balance. To redress it
Bevin and Kingsley Wood were brought into the War Cabinet. Bevin
was certainly an asset on the Labour side but Wood was not strong
enough to sustain the Conservative cause.

A further change came in December after the sudden death of Lord
Lothian, the British ambassador at Washington. After a futile and
indeed foolish attempt to enlist Lloyd George for the post, it was thrust
upon Halifax. With his departure and Chamberlain's death the only
firm checks on Churchill, short of a Labour revolt, were removed.
Eden, who became Foreign Secretary and a member of the War
Cabinet, was a national figure and not primarily a Conservative spokesman. He provided Churchill with a reliable and sometimes a restraining
associate, a man who could be treated as heir presumptive without any
risk that he would try on the crown. Churchill actually nominated Eden
as his successor in case of his own death. His proposed successor in case
both he and Eden were killed was equally without danger. It was Sir
John Anderson, another man who would never snatch the crown nor
indeed ever had any chance of attaining it.

Churchill was curiously isolated from the political world despite his
devotion to parliament. He had been cut off from most Conservatives
during the 1930s. His long experience of politics was shared by no one
except Sir John Simon, now Lord Chancellor as Viscount Simon, and
Simon was by no means one of Churchill's boon companions. Churchill
never developed with Attlee the intimacy that Lloyd George had had
with Bonar Law. Indeed he did not esteem highly any of the Labour
ministers except Bevin. His only intimate in the War Cabinet was
Beaverbrook, and this solely on the grounds of personal friendship.
Otherwise he relied for political guidance on Bracken, who also took
over the direction of public opinion when he became Minister of Information, and for general counsel on Lindemann, later Lord Cherwell,
who counted for more than any member of the War Cabinet. Churchill
himself took great care over his public image both in his appearances
and in his broadcast addresses, but his incursions into parliamentary
debate were those of an elemental force rather than of a routine parlia-
mentarian.

The remodelled War Cabinet survived without serious anxiety

throughout the period when Great Britain stood alone. In December 1940 an ILP motion for a compromise peace was defeated by 341 votes to four and when the Communists took up the same cry the *Daily Worker* was banned without provoking any protest. There was some grumbling about British failures and an unavowed opposition led by Shinwell and Lord Winterton – 'Arsenic and Old Lace' – with Aneurin Bevan providing a one-man imitation of Charles James Fox during the wars against revolutionary France. On the first mutterings of discontent Churchill always defied the critics by demanding a debate in the House. On 7 May 1941, after the British defeats in North Africa, he won a vote of confidence by 477 votes to three and 'an ovation such as he had never yet received'. On 10 June, after the British withdrawal from Crete, there was another debate, though this time no division.

The political atmosphere was sharply changed on 22 June 1941, when the Germans invaded Russia. Churchill at once aligned himself and the country on Russia's side. Some Conservatives would have preferred to let Germans and Russians cut each other's throats and one minister, Moore-Brabazon, lost his post for saying so. Otherwise there was no dispute over Churchill's line. Conservatives acquiesced in support for Russia and most Labour members had little affection for Russia except as a wartime ally. Beaverbrook was Russia's only firm friend in the War Cabinet. The situation was different outside parliament. The Communists were now as enthusiastic for the war as they had previously been opposed to it and their influence was strong in the factories. The idea of a People's War took on practical form for the first time. The Ministry of Information spent many weary hours puzzling how to extol Russian achievements without admitting that Communism had any merits. The Ministry's efforts were not successful. The Internationale had to be admitted to the nightly roll call of Allied anthems on the radio, despite protests from Churchill, and Red Army Day was celebrated everywhere in the presence of mayors, bishops and high-ranking officers on 25 February 1942.

The year 1942 saw the political crisis of the war. The underlying cause was of course the run of disasters in the Far East – two great battleships sunk, Singapore lost, India threatened with invasion. There were two more immediate causes. One was the Left-wing demand for 'a Second Front now' in aid of Russia. The other, more concealed, was the general direction of production. This last provided a striking example of Churchill's tactics and hesitations. For while he had firmly seized the military direction of the war from the first, direction of the civil side was in confusion. The Defence Committee (Supply) was ineffective. The three supply ministries – the Admiralty, the Ministry of Aircraft Production and the Ministry of Supply (for the army) – simply scrambled for everything they could lay their hands on. An overlord of production was the obvious answer but Churchill dared not appoint

one. For such an overlord would be as supreme on the civil side as
Churchill was on the military and therefore a rival near the throne.
Churchill's answer was Beaverbrook, who lacked a political following
of his own. Beaverbrook resisted Churchill's promptings throughout
1941, ostensibly on the grounds of his health, really because he feared
opposition from his colleagues, particularly from Bevin.

The two problems became acute together at the end of January 1942
when Churchill returned from his meeting with President Roosevelt at
Washington. There were underground mutterings in favour of an
independent Minister of Defence, with Churchill retained only as an
oratorical figurehead. He at once challenged these mutterings in a
parliamentary debate and obtained a vote of confidence by 464 to one.
Thus emboldened, Churchill tried again for a Ministry of Production,
now essential in order to co-ordinate British production with that of the
United States. Armed with this new argument, Churchill at last
persuaded Beaverbrook to take the post, which he did on 4 February
1942.

At precisely this moment Sir Stafford Cripps, who had been British
ambassador in Moscow, returned uninvited to London. Cripps enjoyed
wide esteem, altogether undeserved, as the man who had brought Russia
into the war. He had a high, indeed excessive, confidence in his own
abilities. He returned from Moscow with the deliberate intention of
presenting himself as the new national saviour and of ousting Churchill
in 1942 just as Lloyd George had ousted Asquith in 1916. He demanded
to be made Minister of Production with a seat in the War Cabinet.
Churchill would only offer him the Ministry of Supply, subordinate to
Beaverbrook. Cripps refused the offer and went round the country as
the new champion of the Second Front. The industrial workers
responded more eagerly to Cripps than they had done to Beaverbrook,
although he had in fact abandoned his Left-wing views long ago.

Here was a danger for Churchill. The Labour members of the War
Cabinet were also in a quandary. They distrusted Beaverbrook and were
determined not to have him as overlord. They were almost equally cool
towards Cripps but in a sense he was one of themselves and, as they
knew from previous experience, a man who could be tamed, a decoy
duck for the popular discontent. Beaverbrook was the immediate
victim. Inevitably as overlord of production he ran into trouble both
with Bevin, who refused to surrender direction of labour, and with the
Admiralty, which refused to surrender control of shipbuilding.
Churchill, himself threatened, dared not support Beaverbrook and
perhaps, in view of Beaverbrook's advocacy of the Second Front, did
not want to do so. On 18 February Beaverbrook resigned. Churchill
took the opportunity to reconstruct his Cabinet and the results were
startling.

Greenwood, who had proved a failure, was ejected from the War

Cabinet. Ostensibly to balance his going, Kingsley Wood, the only solid Conservative in the War Cabinet, was ejected also. Attlee was officially named as Deputy Prime Minister. Churchill relinquished the Leadership of the House to Cripps, who swallowed the bait and thus secured the limelight instead of the power. The dangerous Ministry of Production went to Oliver Lyttelton, member of a famous Conservative family but himself a businessman with no political experience and therefore not a rival near the throne. The previous respect for a balance between the parties in accordance with their respective strengths in the House was abandoned. Labour, though the minority in the House, provided both the Deputy Prime Minister and the Leader of the House. Attlee was the only party wheel-horse in the Cabinet; all the others were outsiders or former rebels. There was not a single reliable Conservative in the Cabinet. It is not surprising that the Conservatives in the House of Commons became restive.

Things continued to go badly for the government. Between March and June 1942 it lost four by-elections to Independents, all of them demanding a non-party government and a more energetic conduct of the war. On 1 and 2 July 1942, after the fall of Tobruk, there was a vote of no confidence in the House of Commons – a demonstration of hostility never attempted in the First World War. Churchill defeated the motion by 476 votes to 25 with some 30 deliberate abstentions. But his position was insecure. He himself feared that he might fall. According to one rather questionable account, he told Beaverbrook: 'You will be Prime Minister. Nothing can stop it. Events will make you Prime Minister . . . Many of the Ministers will refuse to serve under you . . . But I, Churchill, will serve under you.' In fact Beaverbrook was never a serious rival, if only because of his asthma and nervous tension.

The danger from Cripps was more real. Once in the War Cabinet he concerned himself no more with the Second Front. Instead he demanded a reshaping of the conduct of the war. He wanted a war-planning directorate which would supervise strategy and future operations, leaving the chiefs of staff free for detail and routine orders. Churchill, even if he survived as prime minister, would be pushed aside. Tom Jones, reputed to be a shrewd judge, wrote on 14 August, 'There will be a change in time and inevitably (though possibly after a short interlude) Cripps will be PM.' Cripps moved in for the kill. Early in September he threatened to resign unless his proposals for a war-planning directorate were accepted. But Cripps had missed his tide. He lost control of the House by rebuking members who had shown their boredom during a speech of Churchill's. Churchill asked him to defer his resignation until after the approaching battle. Cripps agreed. Victory at El Alamein brought ruin to Cripps. He resigned from the War Cabinet and not a dog barked at his going. Though he still expected to become prime minister, no one shared this belief. The enthusiasm for him had proved 'a fleeting passion'.

Churchill was now secure. His direction of the war was never challenged again. Even at the worst times he had been saved by the question, 'Who could we put in his place?'. Now no one even asked the question. Herbert Morrison took Cripps's place in the War Cabinet, thus reinforcing Labour orthodoxy there. The faithful Eden succeeded Cripps as leader of the House of Commons. This War Cabinet remained virtually unchanged for the duration of the war. The only newcomers were the Australian Richard Casey, Minister Resident in the Middle East, whose membership was more nominal than real, and Lord Woolton, Minister for Reconstruction, who joined the War Cabinet in November 1943. Woolton was a portent. There was no more controversy over the conduct of the war, though some over foreign affairs. The new disputes were concerned with social policy and the shape of British society after the war, disputes between the parties rather than discontent with the government.

The first preliminary storm came from the Conservatives in May 1942. Dalton and Cripps, both socialists, produced a plan for coal rationing. The Conservatives, always sensitive to anything connected with the mining industry, suspected that this was a socialist plot to smuggle in nationalisation by the back door. The two ministers were much harried in the House and, though there was no hostile vote, the government ran away. Rationing of coal was scrapped. This was the one successful Conservative revolt of the war.

The next storm was more significant. In December 1942 Sir William Beveridge produced his famous plan for universal social security. Churchill did not like it and the Labour members of the War Cabinet loyally supported him. When the plan was presented to the House on 16 February 1943 Sir John Anderson explained that while the government accepted its provisions in principle there could be no binding commitment. An amendment demanding prompt legislation was put forward and defeated only by 338 to 121. With two exceptions all Labour members not in office voted for the amendment. Bevin was so angered by this revolt that he refused to attend meetings of the Parliamentary Labour Party from February 1943 until May 1944.

Another revolt had its comic side. In March 1944 the House of Commons carried by 117 votes to 116 an amendment to the Education Bill demanding equal pay for women teachers – the only occasion in the war when the National Government was defeated on a major question. Churchill was enraged by this defiance. He summoned the leading rebels and insisted that they must recant. The next day he went down to the House and demanded a reversal of the vote. He got his way by a large majority.

Though there were no more open revolts over social policy, back-bench Labour members were clearly asserting a more defined outlook and the Conservatives shrank from opposing them. A further portent was the appearance of a new party, Common Wealth, preaching the idealistic socialism that the Labour leaders were reluctant to formulate. Common Wealth ran candidates at eight by-elections, three of them successfully. These candidates were not the disgruntled critics of earlier years. They expressed the widespread conviction that the People's War should be translated into practical terms.

There was also a rift between the parties over foreign affairs. Though all, or almost all, agreed on carrying the war to a victorious conclusion, the Conservatives wanted to restore old Europe, not to make a new one; some Labour members looked forward to a socialist Europe, based on the Resistance and led by a socialist Great Britain. In December 1944 British troops were sent into action against the Greek Resistance which was mostly Communist-controlled. There were widespread protests in which both *The Times* and the *Manchester Guardian* joined, and a motion of censure in the House of Commons. Though the motion was defeated by 281 votes to 32, only 23 Labour members supported the government – 24 voted against it and the rest abstained. Bevin continued his loyalty to the War Cabinet by declaring at the Labour Party Conference, 'These steps that we have taken in Greece are not the decisions of Winston Churchill, they are the decisions of the Cabinet.' The Greek Resistance was defeated and the Greek monarchy ultimately restored.

On the other side, when Churchill returned from the conference at Yalta, some Conservatives rallied to the cause of pre-war Poland. Twenty-five Conservatives voted against the motion to approve the Yalta agreement and a junior Conservative minister, Henry Strauss, resigned. At the time Churchill remained ostensibly loyal to the Soviet alliance, but his mind was already moving towards the idea of resisting Soviet gains after the war, and this was one of his motives in wishing to continue the coalition. The other and more important motive was to moderate the plans for social reconstruction on which all parties were nominally agreed.

The war against Germany ended on 8 May 1945. Churchill had declared as far back as 31 October 1944 that it would be wrong to prolong the existing parliament, now nearly ten years old, after the defeat of Germany. On the other hand the Japanese war had still to be won – a task which, it was thought, would take another eighteen months. It was also relevant that almost everyone expected Churchill to win a Khaki Election if one were fought immediately. On 18 May Churchill therefore drafted a letter with Attlee's assistance, proposing either that the coalition should be continued until the end of the Japanese war or that there should be an immediate election.

Sinclair, the Liberal leader, wished to continue the coalition. So did Attlee, Bevin and Dalton. Only Morrison was against it. The annual Labour Party Conference was just meeting at Blackpool, and the National Executive Committee of the party recognised that the Conference would insist on rejection, which it did with only two dissentients. In Beaverbrook's words, 'In the inner councils the three were far stronger than the one. But the decision had to be taken while the Socialist Party Conference was meeting at Blackpool, and the Party's rank and file were eager for the fray. So the three generals without an army were beaten by the one general who found an Army to fight with.' Thus the Labour Party Conference which had formally created the National Government by its vote in 1940 ended it with equal formality by its vote in 1945.

Attlee replied to Churchill on 21 May, offering to continue the coalition until October when there should be a general election. Churchill took a straw vote of the Conservative ministers, all of whom favoured an immediate election, for obvious reasons of party advantage. Churchill therefore rejected Attlee's offer and insisted on an election. On 23 May he resigned as National prime minister and a few hours later resumed office as head of a caretaker government, composed of Conservatives and a few ostensibly non-party figures. On 28 May he entertained the leading members of the former government at 10 Downing Street, and said to them, 'The light of history will shine on all your helmets', after which the National Government vanished as though it had never been.

All previous coalitions left wreckage in their train. The creation of Lloyd George's coalition shattered the Liberal party and its dissolution split the Conservatives, though less permanently. Churchill's National Government preserved the existing parties intact. Conservatives might complain that they had been too busy fighting the war to keep the rust off their party machinery It would be truer to say that they lost the general election of 1945 by taking their victory under Churchill's aegis for granted. At any rate the Conservatives soon recovered and the two parties have roughly balanced to the present day.

There was a difference all the same. The cleavage between the two major parties was never as sharp as it had been before the war, whatever harsh words might be exchanged in parliament. The experiences of the war made Labour an acceptable alternative to the Conservatives. Not even Aneurin Bevan was reviled by the Conservatives in the way Lloyd George had been. Attlee and Churchill debated fiercely enough but they also shared the secrets of nuclear warfare behind the scenes. Moreover the disputes over social and foreign policy during the war had not followed rigid party lines. Some Conservatives were as strong as any Labour man for social reform and some also looked forward to co-operation with the Resistance and with Soviet Russia after the war. Tito's firmest advocate was Fitzroy Maclean, a Conservative M.P. Eden was Soviet Russia's friend in the War Cabinet; Attlee was nearest to being her enemy. Hence the post-war disputes over social policy were not much more than synthetic sound and fury, and controversy over relations with Soviet Russia was silenced when Attlee and Bevin took the anti-Soviet line in the Cold War.

Over the greatest issue of all, the Second World War itself, the parties were united from the beginning and remained united until the end. They differed only over details. All could have said with Churchill, 'I have only one aim in life, the defeat of Hitler, and this makes things easy for me'. It is unlikely that there will be another cause uniting all politicians and nearly all Englishmen and, unless one is found, the achievement of Churchill's National Government will remain unique.

# 5 1945–1977

## DAVID BUTLER

In the thirty-two years after 1945 Britain experienced one-party government. But from time to time inter-party deals were mooted, and at last in 1977, following the longest period of unambiguous single-party responsibility that the country had experienced since the Whig supremacy, an explicit arrangement was reached between two parties to keep a minority administration in office. The final chapter of narrative in this book is the least eventful, but its climax illustrates a continuity in British politics: the party understanding of 1977 echoes problems raised by the crises of each of the preceding periods.

The wartime Coalition, that broke up so abruptly on 23 May 1945, had a final burial with Labour's landslide victory in the July election. Wartime bipartisanship was ending with the swift collapse of the Japanese war and the Labour party was determined to rule alone. It had no need to seek allies among the petty parties of the far left, while many of its policies solidified the Liberals in opposition to it.

Over the next decade the only significant moves towards coalition or party alliance came from Winston Churchill. The National and Liberal members of the June 1945 Caretaker Government were defeated in the election or moved over to the Conservatives. But Mr Churchill still hankered after the goal he had sought in the early 1920s, a broad-based anti-Socialist alliance. Soon after he went into opposition he held talks with the official Liberals about the possibility of an electoral pact, offering them a clear run in 60 seats. After this approach came to nothing, he fostered the Woolton–Teviot agreement of May 1947, an understanding between the Chairman of the Conservative Party and the Chairman of the National Liberals. By the 1945 Parliament the National Liberal rump had been reduced to thirteen MPs, two survivors from 1931 and eleven who had succeeded to old National Liberal seats; none, of course, had had Conservative opposition in their constituencies. Following the Woolton–Teviot agreement, some 60 alleged 'Conservative–Liberal' mergers were arranged at the constituency level and in 1950 53 candidates stood under miscellaneous headings, such as Nat. Lib. and Con., Con. and Nat. Lib., Con. and Lib., or Lib. and Con.

The use of these labels provoked much indignation from the official Liberals and their leader, Clement Davies, demanded that 'in the

interests of fair play' Mr Churchill should dissociate himself from some
of the bogus Liberal–Conservative mergers. Mr. Churchill replied:

My dear Davies,

. . . . As you were yourself for 11 years a National Liberal. . . . I
should not presume to correct your knowledge of the moral,
intellectual and legal aspects of adding a prefix or suffix to the
honoured name of Liberal. It has certainly often been done before by
honourable and distinguished men. [However] I have not heard . . .
of any candidate who is standing as a Liberal–Socialist. [For] . . . no
one can be at once a Socialist and a Liberal . . . Why then should you
. . . and your four hundred candidates . . . help the Socialists?. . . .
We hope that serious-minded Liberals will not waste their votes . . .'

But the argument over labels was a very small sideshow in the political
circus. The overwhelming mass of politicians and of electors acted on
the assumption that the political struggle was between Conservative
and Labour.[1]

In 1950 Labour won re-election with a lead of only five seats over all
parties and it was not thought that the government could last for long.
Yet there was no discussion of a Lib–Lab pact, although the nine
Liberals could have raised the majority to 23. But Mr Attlee soon
showed that it was technically possible to retain control of affairs with a
very narrow majority. The Whips were hard-worked, but on every
important division the Government was able to scrape through.
Because it attempted no major legislation, and because it lost no by-
elections, the Labour party survived without any help from the Liberals
for eighteen months.

In October 1951 the Conservatives won by the margin of 17 seats.
The Liberals got only 2½ per cent of the vote and only six seats. But Mr
Churchill did not abandon his courtship of them. He immediately
offered a Cabinet post to Clement Davies. After consulting his party,
Mr Davies reluctantly turned down the offer. Even so the
Conservatives were slow to relinquish the effort to present themselves
as a broad-based coalition. In 1959 34 Conservative supporters still
stood with a 'Liberal' element in their party label and the last pre-war
National Liberal did not leave the House until 1966.

Over the post-war decades the idea of a National coalition was intermittently pursued by Lord Elton and a few other correspondents in *The
Times*, but it received no support from the parties, although the public
seemed to be more receptive. Opinion polls regularly found 40 per cent
or more of the electorate anxious to escape from party politics. In 1967
the proportion recorded by the Gallup Poll as endorsing a coalition
reached 52 per cent.

At the time of the Suez affair the Conservatives had a majority of over 60 in the House of Commons. However, the opponents of the venture believed that enough Conservatives were opposed to it for a makeshift coalition to be formed. Hugh Gaitskell, as Leader of the Opposition, ended his broadcast on 4 November 1956 thus:

> Only one thing now can save the reputation and the honour of our country. Parliament must repudiate the Government's policy. The Prime Minister must resign.
> The Labour party cannot alone achieve this. We are a minority in the House of Commons. So the responsibility rests with those Conservatives who, like us, are shocked and troubled by what is happening, and who want a change. I appeal to them especially. Theirs is a difficult decision, and I want to say to them that our purpose, too, in this matter rises above party. I give them indeed this pledge. We undertake to support a new Prime Minister in halting the invasion of Egypt, in ordering the cease-fire, and complying with the decisions and recommendations of the United Nations. In that way only can the deep divisions in the country on this matter be closed. I appeal to those who can bring this about to act now and save the reputation of our country and the future peace of the world.

This public appeal may have been counter-productive, for the initiative surely had to come from the other side. There certainly were a significant number of Conservatives who felt acutely unhappy about the Government's actions and there were some inter-party soundings. However the will and the numbers to overthrow Sir Anthony Eden and his colleagues were lacking, as Sir Walter Monckton's memorandum on Suez makes plain:

> . . . I was the only member of the Cabinet who openly advised against invasion though it was plain that [others were] . . . troubled about it. . . . Naturally I considered whether I ought to resign. . . . I knew that if I did resign it was likely that the Government would fall, and I still believed that it was better for the country to have that Government than the alternative. What the Labour people had in mind was a kind of rump of the Tory Government led by Butler, which they would support. This could not last.[2]

Sir Walter Monckton recognised the inherent instability of any temporary inter-party arrangement and drew back. But the possibility, as always, was there.

Lord Hailsham writes revealingly on the general problem of party deals, and particularly of Conservative–Liberal deals in his memoirs:

When I was Party Chairman [in 1958–9] I was under very constant pressure from well-meaning persons of various colours to make some sort of deal with the Liberals of that day. Apart from two or three constituencies where ad hoc arrangements were made on a local basis under pressure from the leader of the party, who in this matter had his own interest to pursue, I did not respond to this pressure. Indeed, I could think of no more certain way for a party in office to ensure its own defeat than to be seen to make an arrangement of this kind before holding an election. But, in truth, such an arrangement was not to be made, and what would have done the damage was not the making of it but the fact that I had attempted it. If I had set about it, it would have been necessary first to make an arrangement with the National leadership of the Liberal party and to have persuaded my Cabinet colleagues, the 1922 Committee, which was a body designed to have a will of its own and never slow to take umbrage at the action of the leadership, and the National Union. The terms demanded by the Liberal party would have consisted of two parts, each of which would have presented insuperable difficulties to one or more of these bodies. The first part would have consisted in a demand for some form of proportional representation, probably the single transferable vote. This would have split all these sections of Conservatives, but particularly the Cabinet and the Parliamentary Party, the members of which would have gone scurrying back to their own constituencies to see how far the proposed arrangement would affect their individual chances of survival. The second part of the Liberal demands would have been even more difficult. They would have been driven to suggest that in a given number of seats, say thirty, Conservative candidates would be withdrawn, in return for a promise that in another given number of seats, possibly not the same, Liberal candidates would be withdrawn. This would have been an impossible exercise with virtually no sitting Liberal members, a very large number of sitting Conservative members, and a very limited number of Labour-held seats where either a Liberal or a Conservative candidate had a real chance of getting in. It must be remembered that, on the withdrawal of either a Liberal or Conservative candidate, the votes he would otherwise have got are not automatically transferred. A number of voters would abstain in disgust. A number of Liberals would certainly vote Socialist in the absence of a Liberal candidate, and the corresponding switch would also take place in some areas where there are a number of strong working-class Conservative voters. When it came down to designating the particular constituencies concerned, the task would be impossible unless, between the local Conservative and Liberal associations, there was already a feeling of cordiality sufficient to make the association lined up for sacrifice willing to withdraw its candidate. Such feelings of self-sacrifice cannot normally be imposed from above and, on the level of constituency organisations, nothing can be more disheartening or destructive for years afterwards of morale than such a request coming from national headquarters. Finally, and most ludicrous of all, if all went through up to this point, in a number of cases at least, no sooner would the official candidate be withdrawn than out of the undergrowth an unkempt John the Baptist type figure would emerge calling himself, as the case might be, an Independent Liberal or Conservative, or, in the case of some Welsh and Scottish constituencies, a Nationalist, and carry off all the votes which had been bargained and sold as the result of the arrangement. I think the Conservative party owes me one or two debts of gratitude. But none is more demonstrably owed than this, that I absolutely refused to countenance any negotiations so obviously based on sloppy thinking.[3]

Labour leaders were under less pressure, although in 1961 growing Liberal success in by-elections did lead Woodrow Wyatt, then a Labour M.P., to advocate a Lib–Lab alliance as the best way of ousting the Conservative Government. But his was a relatively lone voice and Mr Gaitskell went out of his way to deride any such tactic, using arguments that were very comparable to Lord Hailsham's.

The 1964 election gave victory to the Labour party – but with an overall majority of four (soon reduced to two by the Leyton by-election). Mr Wilson did not hesitate. In a victory broadcast he said:

The government have only a small majority in the House of Commons. I want to make it quite clear that this will not affect our ability to govern. Having been charged with the duties of Government we intend to carry out those duties.

It is easy to assume that Mr Wilson's decision to govern as though Labour had a larger majority was inevitable. Yet the arguments for caution – for either forming a coalition with the Liberals or trimming the more controversial parts of Labour's programme – were strong. With such a majority it would be all but impossible to get vigorously opposed legislation through, and the country was on the brink of a major economic crisis. However, Mr Wilson must have recoiled from the delays and suspicions that would be involved in any coalition negotiations; he could certainly govern for a few weeks and he could argue that he was only embarking on an experiment; if the experiment failed, he could honourably go back to the country and ask for a proper working majority.

None the less the possibility of a coalition or an understanding was much more actively canvassed then it had been in 1950 when the parliamentary arithmetic was very similar.

|          | Lab | Lib | Other | Con | Total Opposition |
|----------|-----|-----|-------|-----|------------------|
| 1950–51  | 315 | 9   | 3     | 298 | 310              |
| Oct 1964 | 317 | 9   | –     | 304 | 313              |
| Apr 1965 | 316 | 10  | –     | 304 | 314              |

Everyone was aware that the nine or ten Liberals[4] could safeguard Labour's position and, after the loss of Leyton in January 1965, the idea of Lib–Lab talks was certainly on the cards. The Labour party took no formal initiative although, by May, Downing Street was signalling that the Government was concerned about Liberal attitudes and in August, when the opinion polls were at their worst for Labour, there were even hints about the possibility of electoral reform. Certainly indications were given that, in drafting the Queen's Speech for the autumn, the Liberals were in the Government's mind.

But it was left to the Liberals to make the running. They did not like much of what the Government was doing and they feared being blamed for keeping Labour in – but equally they did not want to put the Conservatives back. Mr Grimond set out this familiar dilemma in a little noticed interview in March:

> My view is that either we must have some reasonably long-range agreement with the government or a general election. We must have an agreement for a few months on some purpose we both want.
>
> I should be very much opposed to going back to the 1929 system, in which the Labour government and the Liberal party made practically daily *ad hoc* decisions on the business of government.
>
> I should be very much inclined to say: 'We are in this difficult situation. Here are certain things both parties want to get through. We will support you on all issues, however minor, until that is done.'

He put it a little differently in a more publicised article in the *Sun* in early June:

> If you are living on a small majority it is common sense either to approach the Liberals . . . with proposals for active co-operation, or at least to concentrate your proposals within a range where their support is likely.

Labour's response was to concentrate on mutually acceptable proposals. It was not a very positive line, as Mr Wilson's remarks to the

Party Conference in September indicated:

> I hope that others will feel able to support these measures which we
> put forward because we believe them to be in the national interest. If
> they can we shall welcome their support. If they cannot, we shall have
> to go on without them.

Later he was slightly more forthcoming, telling the *Guardian*:

> But a wide field of our legislative programme ought to – and will, I
> think – fit in with the doctrine, enunciated by the *Guardian*, of
> 'parallel courses'.

When it came to the point, the Liberals were never in a position of
power in the 1964–6 parliament. Moreover the Labour party was never
far enough behind in the opinion polls for Mr Wilson to feel it necessary
to secure a guarantee against being forced into a premature general
election. The parliament lasted long enough for all parties to think
about the problems and costs of any deal – and for the Liberals, in
particular, to experience the internal strains of agreeing on the price
that they would be willing to pay for taking sides.

Labour's decisive victory in 1966 put an end, for the time being, to
such agonising, and Mr Heath's unexpected triumph in 1970 did
nothing to revive the issue. Eight years passed without any significant
discussion of the subject. In 1972–3 power-sharing in Belfast was a
major item on the national agenda but few seem to have applied
analogies from Stormont to Westminster. All parties behaved as
though totally surprised by the situation which the February 1974
election produced.[5]

On 1 March it became plain that for the first time since 1929 the
electoral system had failed to produce a clear majority; moreover,
while minor parties had proliferated to an unprecedented degree, no
single one of them controlled enough seats to give a clear majority to
either of the big parties. Firm government could only be guaranteed by
an understanding between at least three parties. The result that faced
British politicians that afternoon was the most indecisive since the
coming of universal suffrage:

| | |
|---|---:|
| Conservative | 297 |
| Labour | 301 |
| Liberal | 14 |
| S.N.P. | 7 |
| Plaid Cymru | 2 |
| Ulster Unionist | 11 |
| Others | 3 |
| | 635 |

Majority = 318 seats

Mr Wilson was surest in his handling of the situation. His Shadow Cabinet quickly issued a statement saying that 'since the Conservatives have failed in their appeal for an increased majority, they lack the authority to give the lead the country is seeking. Therefore the Labour party is prepared to form a government.' For the next three days Mr Wilson and his colleagues kept a low profile and sought no alliances.

Mr Heath did not resign at once, as he might have done. He argued that, since no party was in a position automatically to form a government, his responsibility as Prime Minister was to see if he could get together an administration that would command a majority. He sent a telegram to the Leader of the Ulster Unionists, offering them the Conservative Whip. But his main focus was on the Liberals. Consultations went on for 72 hours between Mr Heath and Mr Thorpe as well as within the Cabinet and within the Liberal party. But on Monday, 4 March, the fourteen Liberal M.Ps. met and unanimously rejected Mr Heath's offer of a coalition. What had happened is best summarised by the published exchange of letters. Mr Heath wrote to Mr Thorpe:

. . . When we met on Saturday afternoon, we agreed that, . . . the essential and urgent need was that an Administration should be formed which would have sufficient support in the new House of Commons to carry on the Queen's Government. . . .

We noted that the Leader of the Labour Party had issued a statement which made it clear that he would be prepared to form a minority government but not to enter into any coalition or understanding with other parties in the House. . . . I made clear my belief that it would be possible to construct a programme for the Queen's Speech on the opening of Parliament which both the Conservative and the Liberal parties could honourably and in good conscience support. . . .

I told you on Saturday that I thought that from the point of view of the stability and confidence of a new Administration full Liberal participation in government was preferable to other possible arrangements. . . . We are now convinced that full Liberal participation in government, and thus in all the decisions of government, will be essential if we are to ensure a stable Administration. . . We do not think that, on its own, an arrangement for Liberal support would be sufficient . . . You asked what were my views . . . and I told you that I should have to consult my colleagues. I have now done so. . . .

. . . I am authorised to tell you that my colleagues and I in the present Cabinet would be prepared to support the setting up of a Speaker's Conference to consider the desirability and possibility of a change in our electoral arrangements. . . . We should be ready to co-operate in seeing that the conclusions and recommendations of the conference were put to Parliament in the customary way. . . .

Mr Thorpe replied:

> At our meetings on Saturday . . . no commitment of any sort was
> entered into by me, save that I would report our discussions to my
> colleagues. . . .
> . . . on Sunday night, . . . I made it clear that in my view, after
> preliminary soundings, there was no possibility of a
> Liberal–Conservative Coalition proving acceptable but that we
> might give consideration to offering support from the opposition
> benches to any minority government on an agreed but limited
> programme. This you have now explicitly rejected. . . .
> . . . After meeting my parliamentary colleagues in the Commons this
> morning this attitude was confirmed . . . we believe that the only way
> in which the maximum degree of national co-operation can be
> achieved is for a government of national unity to be formed to
> include members of all parties. . . .
> . . . Accordingly I do not believe that a Liberal presence in the
> Cabinet, designed to sustain your Government, would prove
> acceptable. I am glad to note your support for a reference to a
> Speaker's Conference. . . .

In fact nobody, except perhaps Mr Wilson, seems to have thought very
clearly or quickly on that Friday afternoon. At the time the Cabinet
first met several results were still outstanding and it was not even certain
that Labour would end up with more seats than the Conservatives. And
once the Cabinet had launched on the course of consulting the Liberals,
they had to wait until the Liberal M.Ps. could be consulted collectively
after the weekend.

In retrospect the negotiations can be seen as unrealistic for two
reasons. Firstly the Liberals did not hold the balance of power. If all the
14 Liberal M.Ps. had been willing to vote consistently with the
Conservatives the coalition would have had only 311 seats, seven short
of a Parliamentary majority. Secondly it was never on the cards that the
Liberals would sanction a coalition. Even if the Conservatives had been
willing to put through electoral reform – and they never came near to
guaranteeing that – the mass of the Liberal activists and a majority of
the M.P.s would have recoiled from such a deal. The Liberals had just
won 20 per cent of the vote – their greatest success for 45 years: their
advance had been largely at the expense of the Conservatives. And the
Conservative party had just been rebuffed by the British electorate.

Over the weekend Liberal headquarters was swamped with protests
from party workers. The radical anti-Tory mood in the party was
strong and any arrangement with the Conservatives would have

ensured a far-reaching split in the Liberal party. It would have proved politically disastrous for the Liberals to co-operate with either Labour or the Conservatives separately.

Afterwards some Conservative leaders said that the negotiations had been worthwhile in that they placed the blame for installing a Labour government squarely on the Liberals. It is doubtful if the public saw it that way and in any case that was not the object of the exercise at the time it was carried out: it was not designed as a tactical manoeuvre. The Conservative ministers who argued for a deal with the Liberals seriously believed that one could be made and they paid a price for making the endeavour: by trying and failing to form a coalition then, Mr Heath forfeited the claim to be given a chance to do so later on, in the Parliament, should Mr Wilson be defeated in the House of Commons.

One interesting aspect of the negotiations was Mr Heath's insistence that Mr Thorpe should take part in a full coalition rather than merely promise support for an agreed programme. It seems that the constitutional problem of how to consult M.Ps. who were not ministers about the contents of the Budget loomed large in Mr Heath's thinking. In their stances on 'coalition' versus 'agreed programme' Mr Heath was following Mr Churchill in 1951; Mr Thorpe was following Mr Grimond in 1965.

Mr Wilson managed to govern through the spring and summer on a minority basis. His opponents were not keen on an early election and forbore from defeating any significant measures until it was too late for a dissolution before the summer holidays. But no major legislation could be got through the House.

However, the parliamentary arithmetic, as well as the economic crisis, fostered coalition thinking. The Conservatives moved slowly towards the idea of a Government of National Unity while the Liberals engaged in a tense and introverted debate about their attitude towards party alliances. Mr Steel, the Liberal Chief Whip, upset some of his party by advocating, in a broadcast on 25 June, that 'all parties should come together on an agreed programme in the national interest'. Mr Thorpe had to explain to Liberal candidates why, after he had rejected a coalition with the Conservatives in March, he felt that the party should be ready in an economic crisis to join in 'an all-party Government of National Unity for a limited period on the basis of agreed policies'. But the Liberal Assembly in September, on the eve of the election, still had to devote a day to defeating those opposed to any coalition, and the party went into battle with the understanding that the 250-strong Liberal Council would meet the day after the election to guide Liberal M.Ps. on their conduct in any coalition situation.

The Conservatives, shocked by their defeat in February, were eager to escape from the image of 'confrontation' which it had left behind. One approach, developed in policy papers during the summer and gradually accepted by Mr Heath, was a commitment to a Government of National Unity. The September Manifesto ran:

> We will consult and confer with the Leaders of other parties, and with the Leaders of the great interests in the nation, in order to secure for the Government's policies the consent and support of all men and women of goodwill. We will invite people from outside the ranks of our party to join with us in overcoming Britain's difficulties.

As the election advanced, this proposal was amplified with difficulty. The extent to which wider co-operation might go and the people who would be involved were never made clear. Mr Heath did say that nothing would be barred in the post-election discussion, but he was not willing to make the supreme sacrifice of his own personal position, if that were needed. However, he did, two days before the election, bring himself to use the taboo word, coalition: 'the real hope of the British people is that a National Coalition government, involving all the parties, should be formed.'

The election result prevented Mr Heath's approach from being put to the test. It may be dismissed by some as election gimmick, designed to erase the memories of February and to dish the Liberals. It did not remain in the forefront of party policy after Mrs Thatcher had taken over from Mr Heath four months later. None the less, it was a significant innovation. The only previous major party election appeals that had endorsed the idea of coalition were in 1918 and 1931 and they had each sought vindication for a coalition that had already been formed, rather than a mandate for creating one.

In October 1974 the electorate gave Labour a clear majority of seats, but the margin was only three and it was based on a lower percentage of the votes than any victory except that of 1922. Talk of coalition persisted. But there was a great difference between Mr Wilson's majority of three in 1965 and his majority of three in 1975. In 1965 there were only nine minor-party M.P.s, all Liberals; Labour had only 12 seats more than the Conservatives. In 1975 there were 39 minor-party M.P.s under different labels; Labour had 42 more seats than the Conservatives. A government defeat would require not only some Labour defections, or by-election losses, but also a consensus among a very diverse group of Liberals, Nationalists and Ulstermen that, on some key issue, they would all vote with the Conservatives. In the first two years of the Parliament the Government successfully carried through some major controversial legislation.

But the idea of a united approach to national problems soon had a further airing. The campaigns which culminated on 5 June 1975 in the referendum on British membership of the Common Market cut across party lines. The anti-Marketeers never managed to gather their forces into an integrated campaign – and many of them, particularly on the Left, refused to share a common platform. But the pro-Marketeers, assembled under the Britain in Europe (BIE) umbrella, were much more close-knit; all major BIE rallies had spokesmen from each of the three parties and a studiously patriotic non-partisanship permeated their central activities. Early in the campaign reporters, noticing the camaraderie shown on BIE platforms, began to suggest that the whole operation was a rehearsal for a coalition. There were a few barbed exchanges on this theme as the campaign progressed, and there is no doubt that among the pro-Market leaders the experience of working together in committees and press conferences and rallies provided a mutual education for them, teaching them to think carefully what would be embarrassing to the other two parties. Mr Prentice in a much publicised speech on the weekend before the vote said 'I believe our co-operation [in the campaign] has been welcomed by millions . . . who have become fed up with the party dogfight. We must not lose this spirit of unity after June 5.' But the referendum left much less of a legacy than expected. Certainly after the vote there was no continuing movement towards the coalition that some had seen forming under BIE. It should also be noted that Mr Jenkins, near the end of his Westminster career, and Mrs Williams, were the only Cabinet ministers besides Mr Prentice to take a major part in BIE; Mr Wilson, Mr Callaghan and Mr Healey stayed clear of explicitly inter-party activities.

Power-sharing or party understanding came to the fore again in a very different context. By April 1976 one by-election defeat and the desertion of two M.P.s to the Scottish Labour Party, together with John Stonehouse's repudiation of the Whip, had cost the Labour government its formal majority in the House of Commons – and therefore its majority in all Standing Committees. November 1976 saw two more by-election defeats for Labour. The Scottish and Welsh Nationalists had been willing to support the government in the hope that it would fulfil its promises of devolution. But when in February 1977 the defection of Labour backbenchers meant that a majority could not be mustered to enforce the essential guillotine on the Committee Stage of the Devolution Bill, the Nationalist attitude hardened.

On 17 March 1977, the Conservatives put down a motion of censure for 23 March, and the government faced the prospect of defeat. Mr Callaghan had to recognise that, to survive, his administration must secure the support either of the Liberals or of the Ulster Unionists. For four days there were hectic discussions. Mr Callaghan and Mr Foot, the Leader of the House, had several meetings with Mr Steel and Mr Molyneaux.

The Ulster Unionists, despite their old association with the Conservatives and their distaste for much of the government's handling of Northern Ireland, held no particular desire for an election: some at least felt that a change of administration would be for the worse. Above all their deputy leader, Enoch Powell, seemed as averse to Mrs Thatcher as Prime Minister as he had been to Mr Heath. But the government could not give Mr Molyneaux what he demanded – a promise of devolution for Northern Ireland on the model proposed for Scotland, and without any mandatory provision for power-sharing with the Catholics. Such a deal, it was felt, would inevitably escalate violence in the Province; it would also cost the government the support of the two Catholic M.P.s, Mr Fitt and Mr Maguire. What Mr Callaghan did was to promise, unconditionally, a Speaker's Conference to examine Ulster representation at Westminster (with a view to an increase from the current 12 to the 17 or 18 which its population justified). When it came to the point this was enough to allow Mr Powell and two of his colleagues to abstain; although Mr West and other leading Unionists back at home expressed indignation, the Ulstermen at Westminster continued to build on the 'constructive' discussions which they had had with the government before the vote.

If the Unionist price for support was too high, it at first seemed that the Liberal price might prove equally impossible. Mr Steel and Mr Pardoe made public conditions during the weekend of negotiations that seemed unacceptable, at least to the more left-wing members of the Cabinet, and on 21 March, Mr Pardoe firmly predicted failure. However, on the next day Mr Callaghan and Mr Steel agreed terms which the Cabinet approved, reportedly by 20 votes to four –but there were no resignations among the four (Messrs Benn, Shore, Orme and Millan).

During the censure debate Mr Callaghan read out a joint statement prepared with Mr Steel:

We agreed today the basis on which the Liberal Party would work with the Government in the pursuit of economic recovery.

We will set up a Joint Consultative Committee, under the Chairmanship of the Leader of the House which will meet regularly. This Committee will examine Government policy and other issues prior to their coming before the House and Liberal policy proposals.

The existence of this Committee will not commit the Government to accepting the views of the Liberal Party or the Liberal Party to supporting the Government on any issue.

We agree to initiate regular meetings between the Chancellor and the Liberal economic spokesman . . .

We agree that legislation for direct elections to the European Assembly in 1978 will be presented to Parliament in this session . . .

[Full note will be taken of the Liberal commitment to proportional representation and there will be a free vote.]

We agree that progress must be made on legislation for devolution. . . .

We agree that the Government will provide the extra time needed . . . [for a Liberal Bill on homelessness] . . . [and that it will limit the scope of the Bill on direct labour organizations of Local Councils]

We agree that this arrangement between us should last until the end of the present parliamentary session, when both parties would consider whether the experiment has been of sufficient benefit to the country to be continued.

We also agree that this understanding should be made public.

The government had a majority of 24 in the censure debate: the Scottish Nationalists, the two Scottish Labour dissidents, the Welsh Nationalists and five Ulstermen voted with the Conservatives; Labour had in addition to all those who took the Labour Whip (except for one invalid) the thirteen Liberals and the two Irish Catholics – and it benefited by the three Unionist abstentions. All through the summer of 1977 the government continued to retain Liberal support but by July the alliance seemed to wear thin, with the failure to reach a stern incomes policy for 1977–78. However, as Parliament dispersed for the recess, it was announced that the pact would be extended so long as the government kept the threatened 'wage explosion' under control. In a published exchange of letters of 28 July Mr Steel wrote

We have decided to continue co-operation into the next session of parliament for so long as the objectives set out in the Chancellor's statement of July 15 are sustained by the government.

We are agreed that the fight against inflation and unemployment is of paramount national importance and stress the need for both the 12-month gap between pay increases and the limit on the general level of earnings increase to 10 per cent. . . .

We agree to continue the consultative machinery. . . .

We understand that, in the next session of parliament, the government will . . . [stress jobs for school-leavers and help for small businesses; encourage profit-sharing schemes; further the shift from direct taxation; try to get the European Elections Bill through in time; bring in new devolution legislation; help first-time house-buyers; foster a more effective competition policy; improve consumer protection; and pursue legal assistance at public inquiries;

intensify scrutiny of public expenditure and reform the Official Secrets Act]. . . .

The government will continue its consultations with the Liberal party already begun, with a view to determining the priorities in the Queen's Speech . . .

In his reply Mr Callaghan wrote

. . . I agree that we should continue the Consultative Arrangements which we established earlier this year, and which have worked well. These arrangements will preserve the independence and integrity of each of our parties, while enabling us to work together in the next session of parliament.

I confirm the government's position on the particular issues and proposals to which you refer in your letter. . . .

It was made plain that one Liberal M.P., Cyril Smith, dissented from this agreement and that two others, Jo Grimond and David Penhaligon, were against it, yet felt bound by party loyalty.

From the outset the Lib–Lab bargain was widely denounced as a self-interested conspiracy between two parties, equally afraid of facing the electorate. Attacks from the Conservatives were to be expected. But the left wing of the Labour party also was unhappy at 13 Liberals being given a voice on policy that was denied to the 80 M.P.s in the Tribune Group, and the Liberals lost some supporters in the country who thought it wrong to keep the government in office.

Yet the original understanding did work as planned. It could be argued that the Labour party was sacrificing nothing of substance. There was no major legislation that they had any expectation of getting through that Liberals wanted to bar. The limited endorsement of a proportional electoral system for the European Assembly was not likely to produce any results. The minor legislation and administrative concessions to Liberal demands were very minor indeed. Only, perhaps, in terms of 'face' had the government had to pay any substantial price for the security in office which the Liberals gave them.

But had the Liberals got nothing from the deal, except the post-ponement of an unwanted election? They would certainly argue other-wise, partly because they put a higher rating on the concessions won, and still more because they felt they had benefited from their new prominence. After March 1977 the 13 Liberal M.P.s ceased to meet as a group; each had a Shadow portfolio and they joined with a few peers to form a Liberal Shadow Cabinet. They had the gratifying experience of regular and, in some cases, intimate discussion with the ministers and officials they were shadowing. After all the years in the wilderness they were at last, albeit in a vicarious way, savouring some of the satisfaction of office. The Consultative Committee – three Liberals meeting weekly with three senior ministers – worked fairly smoothly and offered some insight into and influence on government tactics; occasionally its disagreements had to be referred up to Mr Callaghan and Mr Steel for settlement.

Of course, there were difficulties, perhaps most of all over the way in which the whole operation was to be presented: was it to be seen as a harmonious and mutually profitable partnership, or could either side boast of what they had wrested from the other by tough bargaining? In the initial state at least the advocates of the harmonious interpretation tended to prevail. What was not clear was how each side regarded the sanctions behind the understanding. Obviously the Liberals could bring the government down; obviously the government could force the Liberals into an unwanted early election. But could one envisage either side actually invoking such self-destructive deterrents? Any confrontations between the participants must have been recognised as largely bluff. But not entirely. The government might fix some arrangement with the Ulster Unionists (or even with the Scottish Nationalists) which would render Liberal support unnecessary; it might conclude that some Liberal price would be too high to be tolerated by their rank-and-file; it must also have been aware that, as a five-year parliament advanced, the value of putting off an election diminished. But the Liberals, too, were a little less desperate to avoid an election than some analysts suggested; all the thirteen Liberal M.P.s had a strong local base; as populist independents they might each in their own constituency withstand a collapse of the party's vote nationally. Furthermore the mere fact of the national understanding might educate the anti-Conservative electorate and induce Labour supporters to vote tactically in the few seats which a Liberal challenger had a chance of winning. And, despite the cynics, politicians are not wholly devoid of pride and self-respect. They can get themselves or others into positions from which there is no going back, where there is no option but to pull down the pillars of the Temple, however self-destructively. An awareness of this seems to have permeated the Lib–Lab negotiations. A bargain was struck and implemented between the government and the Liberals in a cautious manner which showed that each side had a due awareness of each other's strength and of the limits of the acceptable for each of them.

It is premature to evaluate the party understanding of 1977. It fell far short of coalition. It took place in a time of economic crisis but it was born of parliamentary tactics rather than national necessity. It was not the child of war, as in 1915 or 1940 and it was not a reaction to a fear of imminent national disaster, as in 1931. It had more in common with the MacDonald–Lloyd George talks of 1930, or even some of the manoeuvres after 1846, when party survival stood out as the motivating force. But in 1977, as in the earlier instances, considerations of national interest were not wholly absent: politicians can easily convince themselves that the success of their principal opponents is the worst disaster that can befall the country. In March 1977 most Labour and Liberal M.P.s believed that an immediate election would bring a Conservative landslide and that the consequences of a government under Mrs Thatcher would be a dismantling of the incomes policy, a serious cut in the social services and a ruinous confrontation with the unions. Conservatives could argue that all these were equally likely if Mr Callaghan stayed in office – but the fact remains that initially at least the pact was welcomed by many middle-of-the-road commentators and, to a remarkable degree, by the Stock Exchange.

By the time of the party Conferences at the end of September national and party fortunes had changed. The economy looked far healthier and the Conservatives no longer had an overwhelming lead in the polls. The pact had plainly cost the Liberals some support yet their Assembly at Brighton gave it a clear-cut endorsement. The Labour Conference did not discuss the matter explicitly but there was no doubt that the party and the Government were happy at the continuance in office and at the enhanced prospects which the deal had made possible.

# 6 Conclusion

## DAVID BUTLER

Single-party government is the British norm. Politicians and writers on politics assume that, in all but exceptional circumstances, one party will have a Parliamentary majority and will conduct the nation's affairs. But those exceptional circumstances have been the subject of this book and before reflecting upon them it is worth setting the record in perspective. In fact clear-cut single party government has been much less prevalent than many would suppose. The years from 1945 to 1974 have coloured contemporary thinking but, even with their inclusion, governments relying on a majority drawn only from a single party have held office for less than half the twentieth century.

|                   |                | Years | Months |
|-------------------|----------------|-------|--------|
| Nov 1922—Nov 1923 | Conservative   | 1     | —      |
| Oct 1924—May 1929 | Conservative   | 4     | 7      |
| July 1945—Oct 1951 | Labour        | 6     | 3      |
| Oct 1951—Oct 1964 | Conservative   | 13    | 0      |
| Oct 1964—June 1970 | Labour        | 5     | 8      |
| June 1970—Feb 1974 | Conservative  | 3     | 8      |
| Oct 1974—Apr 1976 | Labour         | 1     | 6      |
|                   |                | 35 years | 8 months |

To these governments might well be added four more, one in which the component parties were moving towards fusion and three in which one party had a clear majority and was overwhelmingly predominant.

|                   |                                                          | Years | Months |
|-------------------|----------------------------------------------------------|-------|--------|
| July 1900—Dec 1905 | Conservative—Liberal Unionist                           | 5     | 5      |
| Jan 1906—Jan 1910 | Liberal with clear majority (but with Labour and Irish Nat. support) | 4     | 0      |
| Sep 1932—May 1940 | National Government (but with Conservative clear majority) | 7     | 8      |
| May 1945—July 1945 | Caretaker Government (but with Conservative clear majority) | 0     | 2      |
|                   |                                                          | 17 years | 3 months |

There were three periods where there was a clear and explicit coalition government.

|  |  | Years | Months |
|---|---|---|---|
| May 1915–Nov 1922 | Wartime coalition (which con-tinued under a Liberal P.M. after the Conservatives had won a clear majority in Dec 1918) | 7 | 6 |
| Aug 1931–Sep 1932 | National government (a genuine coalition for so long as the Liberals supported it, even after the Conservatives won a clear majority in Oct 1931) | 1 | 1 |
| May 1940–May 1945 | Wartime coalition (genuine despite a clear Conservative majority) | 5 | 0 |
|  |  | 13 years | 7 months |

Finally there were six periods of minority rule, where the government's continuation in office depended on the votes or the abstention of at least one opposition party.

|  |  | Years | Months |
|---|---|---|---|
| Jan 1910–May 1915 | Liberals, dependent on Irish Nationalists (they also had Labour support) | 5 | 4 |
| Jan 1924–Oct 1924 | Labour, dependent on Liberals | – | 8 |
| May 1929–Aug 1931 | Labour, dependent on Liberals | 2 | 2 |
| Mar 1974–Oct 1974 | Labour, dependent on all other parties not uniting to defeat them | – | 7 |
| Apr 1976–Mar 1977 | Labour, dependent on all other parties not uniting to defeat them | – | 11 |
| Mar 1977– | Labour, with agreed Liberal support | – | 9 (to Dec 1977) |
|  |  | 10 years | 5 months |

Thus, over 77 years, Britain has spent 24, almost one third of the time, under coalition or minority governments. It is likely to spend even more time under such rule in the future. The forces that have given the country predominantly single-party government have weakened. There has been a breakdown in the national homogeneity and the voter discipline which induced the nation to fit into a stable two-party mould.

And the electoral system, which has so consistently turned minorities of votes into majorities of seats, is at least under some challenge.

In the last decade the ascendancy of the United Kingdom parties has disappeared in Ulster and significantly diminished in Scotland and, to a lesser degree, in Wales. Between 1945 and 1974 (the longest continuous period of clear-cut majorities) there were on average only 13 M.P.s in each Parliament who did not belong to the Conservative or Labour parties. In four of the eight Parliaments in this period, the government had an overall majority of 30 or less. But in the two elections of 1974, 37 and then 39 minor-party M.P.s came to Westminster; a comparable upsurge in previous elections would have sufficed to give the country minority government in half the post-war parliaments. It would be a bold man who predicted that the United Kingdom would ever revert to the situation that prevailed from 1950 to 1970 when over 98 per cent of M.P.s were attached to one of two parties; despite close elections in 1950, 1951, 1964, and 1970, the residue of M.P.s (almost all Liberal) never held the balance of power – nor, if they had done so, were they ever numerous enough to give a government any lasting guarantee against losing office through the normal incidence of by-elections.

The new threat to the alternating monopoly of power enjoyed by the two big parties has not come solely from regional parties in Scotland, Northern Ireland, and Wales. It has also come from the growing volatility and independence of the voter, manifested in various ways. At a local level, since 1970 there have been three instances of rebel M.P.s defeating official party candidates (something that had not happened since 1945) while a few independents have saved their deposits in situations where they would have had no hope fifteen years earlier. Nationally the jump in the Liberal vote from 7.5 per cent in 1970 to 19.3 per cent in February 1974 was double the biggest change in party support recorded between 1945 and 1970. Equally the collapse in the Conservative vote (—8.6 per cent) and the Labour vote (—5.9 per cent) had no post-war precedent. In every contest from 1945 to 1970 the Conservative and Labour parties each secured between 40 per cent and 50 per cent of the national vote (both averaging 45–6 per cent) but in February 1974 and again in October 1974 both fell below 40 per cent. The two-party monopoly of votes, and even more of seats, was near to being broken. At the very least the majoritarian electoral system had shown an unsuspected capacity to produce indeterminate results.

There followed suggestions that the electoral system which had so often turned the leading party's minority of the national vote into a clear parliamentary majority might not be immutable. Any form of proportional representation must greatly reduce the likelihood of single-party majorities. A change in the system may not be imminent, but since 1974 the idea has been more seriously discussed and has attracted weightier advocates than for half a century. The major parties remain officially opposed to change, but many people, including a proportion of the Conservative front bench, have come to see proportional representation as the surest bulwark both against the uncertainties and reversals of policy caused by complete government overturns, and against the possibility of an irreversible shift of power being brought about by a socialist government with under 40 per cent of the vote.

As indecisive election results become more likely, the possible responses to them and the consequences of those responses become more important. In the past, coalitions have tended to be seen as temporary expedients to cope with a war or a crisis that would not last long; the assumption has been that the next election would offer a clear-cut majority. But once it is accepted that elections are not likely to yield unequivocal verdicts, party deals change their nature; in such circumstances, coalitions become a permanent feature of political life, and if the country is to have stable government, politicians and electorate alike will have to come to terms with the costs and compromises necessary to the working of coalitions.

All textbooks on British government refer to the role of the Monarch in the formation of governments. But for single-party governments, that function came to an end in 1965 with the Conservatives' switch to electing their leader. In coalition situations, the Head of State still has a role to play in summoning successive candidates to try to form a government and, perhaps, in assuming the role of honest broker, discovering routes towards a compromise. The experiences of the President of the Fourth Republic and of the President of Italy offer ample illustrations of this activity. But in this century the British sovereign has not been a major actor in the formation of governments – the only case where the royal role may have been significant was George V's pressure on Ramsay MacDonald to head the National Government. And in most foreseeable crises, it seems probable that the Palace will be presented with a *fait accompli*, its only function being to endorse a deal worked out in the corridors of Westminster. Yet in a complete deadlock, someone might have to mediate, or at least to interpret the ground-rules. The Monarch does not want to get involved in political controversy; constitutional evolution has seen almost every royal exercise of power reduced to a prescribed routine – but there remain areas where no routine has been established. If no group of parties commands a majority and the outgoing prime minister offers no advice, it may be left to the Palace to decide the sequence in which party leaders shall be asked to try to form a government. It may also be left to the Palace to decide who can demand a dissolution; this is certainly not a right that can be granted to anyone who is given an exploratory commission, but does it belong to any prime minister who, after forming a government, fails at the first vote in the House of Commons? If we envisage a world in which elections are unlikely to produce clear-cut decisions, the right to inflict an election on the nation must presumably be limited by agreed rules. A repetition of ambiguous, multi-party situations will necessitate a further codification of constitutional practice. At the moment there are many points where everyone – the Crown, the politicians, the courts, the constitutional experts – are unclear on what the rules of the game should be.

This book is primarily a work of British history, a description and analysis of actual coalitions or party understandings over the last two hundred years. It makes no sortie into the pure theory of coalitions, a well-advanced branch of game theory.[1] Nor does it explore the sophisticated routines by which countries with a continuous experience of coalitions have solved their party crises.

Each of the British coalitions or party understandings has been *sui generis*, arising out of particular parliamentary or national situations. They have varied from enduring partnerships to very short-term promises of support on specific measures. Being so few and so different, they cannot form the subject of much confident generalisation. The rules of the coalition game have to be learnt afresh by the participants each time. Britain has no ritual conventions of negotiation and of power-sharing of the sort developed in the formation and maintenance of governments in the Third and Fourth Republic or in contemporary Holland or Italy.

But some generalisation is possible. Parties join coalitions, or make deals to keep governments in office for diverse reasons: they want a share of power; or they want colleagues who will legitimise unpopular measures; or they are anxious about their electoral survival; or they see a patriotic necessity. But in entering such arrangements they must always have misgivings. Will they suffer from guilt by association with a traditional enemy? Will they lose their party identity? Will they be exposed to intolerable internal strains, perhaps to the point of splitting? Will they be outflanked by ideological purists who reject any truck with the compromises of government? Will they win an adequate share of offices – and of patronage? Will they, in a situation where they can be only partly responsible for what the government does, get sufficient of their own party policy implemented to compensate for all the unpopularity of power? Will the whips be able to deliver the back-bench vote of the other party in support of newly-agreed measures which it once opposed?

In the politics of a coalition the most important fact is, usually, its temporary nature (if it proves enduring, it is likely to lead to a fusion of the partners). What are the conditions for its survival or its break-up? If the objective is to win a war or to surmount a major crisis, external events may provide a cement for the arrangement and define its duration. A coalition that comes into being simply because government must be carried on with the consent of some sort of parliamentary majority will have less stability. But the shadow of the next election must hang, in greater or less degree, over all coalitions. Partisan ministers must be aware that some of the colleagues with whom they are co-operating in running the country are likely to be their adversaries when they next face the voters. When will it be expedient to bring down the government? How far will they be able to claim credit for the government's achievements and place the blame for its failures on others? How far, without destroying the working efficiency of government, can they inform the media, and thus the electorate, of their own faction's beneficial influence in the day-to-day compromises in Cabinet?

A coalition is like an incomes policy, easier to establish in a moment of crisis than to escape from gracefully. As time passes the strains are likely to grow and, when the hour comes for it to end, the *status quo ante* proves impossible to re-establish. Mere participation in a coalition must change each party's image. Coalitions or party deals do, indeed, require an especially sophisticated public, if politicians are to be kept to a sense of answerability. In a single-party government, there is no ambiguity about which party is responsible for the state of the country. But coalitions blur the situation. The political journalist, let alone his readers, may have difficulty in assessing how each side played its cards in reaching a compromise. The rational elector is bound to hesitate in deciding which of the governing partners has earned his support or his censure.

It is, of course, true that the large parties have always been coalitions within themselves; each has developed its own traditions of balance and compromise and has given its leaders a party education in the art of the possible. But there is a fundamental difference between inter- and intra-party arrangements. The deals that take place between rival parties are necessarily more public and excite more suspicion especially among the extra-parliamentary activists. There will always be a tendency to handle at arm's length someone who, before long, is likely to be an opponent in electoral debate.

A coalition operates differently in different arenas – in Cabinet, in Parliament, in the party machines, and in the constituencies. Cabinet necessities are not always understood by the rank and file. The ordinary voter's cynicism about politicians is likely to be enhanced by the manoeuvring – and, indeed, the posturing – that is inevitable in the process of reconciling, publicly, conflicting party interests. If a coalition is to succeed at all, there must be a reasonable working relationship at the top, based on some degree of trust. The further from the centre of affairs, the less likely there is to be understanding or sympathy between the rival partisans whose leaders are locked together in the exercise of power.

Coalition formation cannot be a mechanical exercise, a mere statistical reflection of the parliamentary numbers of its components. As these pages have shown, personalities like Joseph Chamberlain,

Lloyd George, Winston Churchill and even Ramsay MacDonald need their special accommodation. A single refusal to serve may render the whole enterprise impossible and, as 1852 and 1931 illustrated, a minority that is indispensable can secure a disproportionate share of offices.

But coalitions between two unequal parties can turn out to be like the relationship between the tiger and the young lady of Riga. The electorate may soon prove unable to distinguish between the parties: the lesser fry may quickly lose their identity, and with that their goodwill and their electoral base (as the smaller parties in the National Government did after 1931). A lasting coalition of independent partners may, of course, be possible if the component parties come from distinct geographic bases (as with the Liberal–Country Party coalition that has dominated Australian politics for a generation). Equally it is possible for a coalition to have some durability and for its components to maintain their independence if the electoral system is suitably designed (as with the Fine Gael–Labour Party coalition in Ireland or the successive coalitions through which the Free Democrats have managed to share in the government of Germany).

Coalitions are not good or bad. In some countries they are the unavoidable norm. In Britain they are expedients by which government may be continued until a war is won, a crisis is past, or a one-party majority is restored. They may have the special virtue of adding legitimacy to government action: a party that, although possessed of a parliamentary majority, has been backed by only 40 per cent of voters has less moral authority for imposing unpopular measures on the country than a united group of parties which between them received the support of 60 per cent — or perhaps 90 per cent — of voters. Coalitions are devices for reducing the costs of adversary politics, based on governments of alternating parties whose *raison d'étre* lies in disproving each other's solutions.[2] They enable the nation to reach beyond one party for leadership or for administrative skill. They mute factious point-scoring. They encourage the pursuit of national consensus.

But coalitions threaten the disciplines of party. They damp down the organised criticism of government action. They obscure the clear-cut choices of a two-party system. The more all-embracing and successful their composition, the less alternative they leave: dissenters may be driven to extremes.

Coalitions may be necessary; they may solve particular problems; they may save particular parties. But they are seldom ideal. As the French Premier, André Tardieu said, 'Life is one long *pis aller*. So is politics.' We have to make our choice of the least bad alternative. Mere survival, the avoidance of national disaster – or even of party disaster – may be a not unworthy achievement.

# Notes

CHAPTER 1    1783-1902

1. Quoted from Bowood MSS by L. G. Mitchell, *Charles James Fox and the Disintegration of the Whig Party* (1971).
2. 'So ends the great controversy of Free Trade', Gladstone noted in his diary on 26 November. M. R. D. Foot and H. C. G. Matthew (eds), *The Gladstone Diaries* (1973) vol. iv, p. 471.
3. *The Gladstone Diaries*, iv, p. 478.
4. The best account of the birth, life and death of the Aberdeen Coalition is by Professor J. B. Conacher, *The Aberdeen Coalition 1852-55* (1968). I have drawn heavily upon it for this essay. See also C. H. Stuart, 'The Formation of the Coalition Cabinet of 1852' *Trans. R. Hist. Soc.*, 5th series iv (1954), 45-68.
5. A. C. Benson and Viscount Esher (eds) *The Letters of Queen Victoria, 1st Series* (1907) ii, pp. 500—2, Memorandum by Prince Albert, 18 December 1852.
6. See John Prest, *Lord John Russell* (1972) pp. 345-7 for an entertaining account of Russell's administrative incompetence as prime minister. Apart from that, his promotion of the Ecclesiastical Titles Bill made him anathema to the Peelites.
7. Prest, op. cit., p. 354 and Conacher, op. cit., p. 127.
8. Conacher, op. cit., p. 35.
9. Loc. cit. p. 36.
10. Quoted Conacher, op. cit., p. 7.
11. Quoted Conacher, op. cit., p. 39 n1.
12. Roger Fulford, *The Prince Consort* (1949) p. 149, quoting from the Royal Archives.
13. Conacher, op. cit., p. 124.
14. *Letters of Queen Victoria 1st Series* (1907) iii p. 127.
15. Viscount Canning, hitherto Postmaster General without a seat in the Cabinet, had been asked to join it by Palmerston.
16. The Gladstone Diaries published so far end in 1854. It will be interesting, when the next two volumes appear, to see what Gladstone had to say in detail about this curious transaction. There is a brief account in John Brooke and Mary Sorensen (eds), *Prime Ministers' Papers: W. E. Gladstone, 1: Autobiographica* (HMSO, 1971, published under the auspices of the Royal Commission on Historical Manuscripts) pp. 82-3.
17. Arthur Ponsonby, *Henry Ponsonby, His Life from his Letters* (1940) pp. 199-200.
18. See Denis Judd, *Radical Joe* (1977) pp. 137-9, for a discussion of Chamberlain's motives.
19. Lady Gwendolen Cecil, *Life of Robert Marquis of Salisbury*, vol. iii (1931) p. 300.

20. See above p. 6.
21. Salisbury to Hicks Beach, 24 July 1886, quoted Lady Gwendolen Cecil, op. cit., p. 310.
22. Viscount Chilston, *Chief Whip* (1961) p. 84.
23. Quoted Denis Judd, op. cit., p. 173.
24. His chances were wrecked by the extreme longevity of Lord Halsbury, who first became Tory Lord Chancellor in 1885 when he was 62 and only left office when Balfour resigned in 1905. He was still active in politics as leader of the 'Diehards' in 1911.
25. R. C. K. Ensor, *England 1870–1914* (1936) p. 267.
26. Quoted J. L. Garvin, *The Life of Joseph Chamberlain*, vol. iii (1934) p. 613.
27. Denis Judd, op. cit. p. 173.
28. The chance even so was not good, for the Irish Members, as Roman Catholics, were likely to support the measure.
29. *Parliamentary Reminiscences and Reflections 1886–1906* (1922) p. 315.
30. Denis Judd, op cit. p. 186.
31. Quoted, Julian Amery, *Life of Joseph Chamberlain* (1969) vi, p. 973.

CHAPTER 2   1902-1924

1. *The Times*, 8 December 1919.
2. *Labour Leader*, 15 February 1902.
3. R. A. Rempel, *Unionists Divided* (Newton Abbot, 1972) p. 144.
4. His memorandum is printed in Kenneth O. Morgan, *The Age of Lloyd George* (London, 2nd edition, 1975) pp. 150–5.
5. Robert Blake, *The Conservative Party from Peel to Churchill* (London, 1970) p. 195.
6. J. Wedgwood to MacDonald, 12 June 1913 (PRO 30/69, 5/23); memorandum in MacDonald Papers (30/69, 8/1); ILP National Administrative Council minutes, 17 March 1914 (London School of Economics library).
7. Bodleian, Asquith Papers, vol. 26, ff. 12–38.
8. Edward David, 'Charles Masterman and the Swansea District By-Election', *Welsh History Review*, V, no. 1 (June 1970) 31 ff.
9. Runciman to Chalmers, 7 February 1915, cited in C. Hazlehurst, *Politicians at War* (London, 1971) p. 142.
10. John Stubbs, 'The Impact of the Great War on the Conservatives', in G. Peele and C. Cook (eds), *The Politics of Reappraisal, 1918–1939* (London, 1975) p. 26.
11. Asquith to Lloyd George, 25 May 1915, cited in Kenneth O. Morgan, *Lloyd George Family Letters, 1885–1936* (Cardiff and Oxford, 1973) pp. 178–9.
12. Bodleian, Asquith Papers, vol. 26, f. 30.
13. Derby to Sir P. Sassoon, ? 1917, cited in R. Churchill, *Lord Derby, King of Lancashire* (London, 1959) pp. 281–2.
14. Cabinet Committee on War Policy, June 1917 (Bodleian, Milner Papers, box 125, ff. 102–14).
15. Kerr to Lloyd George, 20 November 1918 (H. of Lords Record Office, Ll. G. Papers, F89 / 1 / 13).

16. Guest to Lloyd George, 17 May 1918 (Ll. G. Papers, F21/2/22).
17. Younger to J. C. C. Davidson, 2 December 1918 (H. of Lords Record Office, Bonar Law Papers, 95 / 4).
18. Guest to Lloyd George, 29 October 1918 (Ll. G. Papers, F21/2/46).
19. Notes of a conference held at 12 Downing Street, 19 July 1918 (Bodleian, Addison Papers, box 72).
20. Salisbury to Selborne, 30 August 1918 (Bodleian, Selborne Papers, I, 7, ff. 50–1).
21. Mond to Bonar Law, 8 November 1918; Law to Mond, 15 November 1918 (Bonar Law Papers, 95/3).
22. F. Seymour Cocks to Sir Arthur Ponsonby, 29 December 1918 (Bodleian, Ponsonby Papers, MS Eng. Hist. c. 667, f. 114).
23. Bonar Law to Balfour, 5 October 1918 (B.M., Add. MSS. 49, 693, ff. 272–80).
24. Lord Beaverbrook, *Men and Power, 1917–1918* (London, 1956) p. 325.
25. Contained in Lloyd George Papers, F/35/1.
26. Public Record Office, CAB 26 1–2 (HAC); Churchill to Lloyd George, 6 July 1922 (Ll. G. Papers F/10/3/15).
27. *The Times*, 21 November 1921.
28. Fisher to Lloyd George, 16 November 1920 (Ll. G. Papers, F/16/7/61): Addison's memorandum, 13 April 1921 (CAB 24/122), CP 2829.
29. Cabinet conclusions, 28 March 1922 (CAB 23/29).
30. Cf. Selborne to Salisbury, 13 June 1921 (copy) (Selborne Papers, I, 7, 103–5); Salisbury to Law, 4 March 1922 (Bonar Law Papers, 107/2/21).
31. Balfour's memo. of a conversation with Bonar Law at Whittinghame, 22 December 1922 (B.M., Add. MSS. 49,693, ff. 300–5).
32. *Lloyd George Liberal Magazine*, October 1920, p. 12.
33. Bonar Law to Younger, ? October 1919 (Bonar Law Papers, Box 96/1).
34. Cabinet conclusions, 4 June 1920 (CAB 23/21).
35. Hilton Young to Sir E. Grigg, 23 March 1922 (Bodleian, Grigg papers); Derby's speech to Manchester Constitutional Club (*The Times*, 16 January 1922).
36. Bonar Law to Lloyd George, 27 January 1919 (Ll. G. Papers, F 30/3/7).
37. Sir Robert Sanders to Younger, 2 December 1920; Walter Long to Bonar Law, 8 May 1920 (Bonar Law Papers, 99/8/4; 102/5/16).
38. Guest to Lloyd George, 15 and 17 January 1920 (Ll. G. Papers, F 22/1/3–5).
39. Younger to Bonar Law, 22 January 1921, cited in Beaverbrook, *The Decline and Fall of Lloyd George* (London, 1963), p. 243.
40. H. A. L. Fisher's diary, 4 February 1920 (Bodleian, Fisher Papers).
41. Bonar Law to Balfour, 24 March 1920 (Bonar Law Papers, 96/4).
42. E.g. *The Nation*, 25 February 1922.
43. Lord Robert Cecil to J. A. Spender, 30 August 1921 and to W. Runciman, 2 September 1921 (B.M., Add. MSS 51,163, ff. 12–16).
44. Sutherland to Lloyd George, 3 September 1922 (Ll. G. Papers, F35/1/55).
45. The present writer is currently writing on this theme in *The Making of Post-war Britain, 1918–22*, to be published by Oxford University Press.
46. *The Times*, 7 October 1922 (letter from Bonar Law).
47. Trevor Wilson, *The Downfall of the Liberal Party, 1914–1935* (London, 1966) p. 237.
48. Cabinet conclusions, 20 November 1945 (PRO, CAB 128/2). The discussion concerned housing policy.

49. L. Worthington-Evans to Austen Chamberlain, 22 May 1923 (Bodleian, Worthington-Evans, Papers, box 6).
50. This is discussed in David Marquand's excellent *Ramsay MacDonald* (London, 1977) pp. 238 ff.


CHAPTER 3   1924-32

1. David Marquand, *Ramsay MacDonald* (1977) pp. 311–12.
2. Ibid., p. 289.
3. W. L. Guttsman, *The British Political Elite* (1963) pp. 237–42.
4. Marquand, op. cit., p. 529.
5. Ibid., p. 531.
6. Cabinet 68 (30).
7. Marquand, op. cit., p. 584.
8. Ibid., p. 593.
9. Frank Owen, *Tempestuous Journey: Lloyd George, His Life and Times* (1954) p. 717.
10. Marquand, op. cit., p. 631.
11. Ibid., pp. 655–6.
12. R. Bassett, *Nineteen Thirty-One* (1958) p. 188.
13. David Wrench, 'Aspects of National Government Policy', University of Wales Ph.D. thesis, p. 30.
14. Marquand, op. cit., p. 655
15. Wrench, op. cit., p. 34.
16. MacDonald to George V, 14 September 1931 (MacDonald papers, 5/43).
17. Diary entry, 18 September 1931 (MacDonald papers, 8/1).
18. Usher to MacDonald, 23 September 1931 (MacDonald papers, 5/43).
19. Marquand, op. cit., pp. 661–2; Robert Rhodes James, *Memoirs of a Conservative* (1969) p. 375.
20. Harold Nicolson, *King George V* (1952), p. 491.
21. Cabinet 70 (31).
22. Earl of Avon, *The Eden Memoirs: Facing the Dictators* (1962) p. 23.
23. Cabinet 47 (32).
24. Philip, Viscount Snowden, *An Autobiography* (1934), vol. 2, pp. 1026–7.


CHAPTER 4   1932-1945

1. I have not given references for the statements of fact in this chapter. Most of the details can be found in *The Road to 1945* by Paul Addison (1975), to whom I am very grateful, and the rest in *English History 1914–1918* by A. J. P. Taylor (revised edition, 1976).
2. The objection to Chamberlain is easy to understand. But why Simon? Was it his conduct during the Manchurian affair? Or his later acts as Chancellor of the Exchequer? Perhaps only that he was a symbol of the National pretence as leader of the Liberal National party.
3. Kingsley Wood has also been given the credit for saying to Churchill, if he were asked to serve under Halifax, 'Don't agree and don't say anything'. In my opinion this belated recollection by Eden was an unconscious transference of credit from Bracken to Wood.

4. Churchill (*The Second World War*, vol. I, p. 543) transfers Halifax's remarks about his peerage to another conversation on the morning of 10 May. According to Churchill's account, Chamberlain told him that he was to be prime minister and he replied that he would have no communication with either of the opposition parties until he held the King's Commission to form a government. It is difficult to see when this conversation took place. In any case Chamberlain knew from the conversation of 9 May (*a*) that he would probably have to resign and (*b*) that Halifax was reluctant to succeed him. No doubt Halifax would have given way if pressed. Significantly Chamberlain did not press him.
5. Churchill took over most of those who had been leading ministers in the preceding government. The only exception was Sir Samuel Hoare and this seems to have been his own choice. He had always been reluctant to work with or under Churchill. Moreover he expected to become the next Viceroy of India and went as ambassador to Madrid in order to keep himself free for this post. The only clear exclusion that Churchill operated was of those ministers, such as Walter Elliot, who had been against the Munich agreement and yet did not resign as Duff Cooper had done.
6. Technically Halifax also remained a member of the War Cabinet throughout the war, but as he was ambassador in Washington from December 1940 onwards this membership became little more than honorary.
7. An Act prolonging the life of parliament cannot be carried by the machinery of the Parliament Act. This is perhaps a justification for preserving the House of Lords.

CHAPTER 5   1945-1977

1. In Huddersfield in 1949 and in Bolton in 1951, pacts were arranged by which the Liberals and Conservatives each gave the other a clear run in one of each town's two seats. These understandings resulted in the Liberals having two extra seats throughout the thirteen years of Conservative rule but it did not set the pattern for any further arrangements.
2. Lord Birkenhead, *Walter Monckton* (London, 1969).
3. Lord Hailsham, *The Door Wherein I went* (London, 1975).
4. In a by-election in March 1965 the Liberals won Roxburgh from the Conservatives.
5. It is true that at the Liberal Assembly in September 1973, John Pardoe did secure a study group to consider coalition possibilities. But nothing had been decided by February 1974.

CHAPTER 6   Conclusion

1. But see T. Schelling, *The Strategy of Conflict* (1958); J. Buchanan and G. Tullock, *The Calculus of Consent* (1962); W. H. Riker, *The Theory of Political Coalitions* (1962); S. Groennings *et al.*, *The Study of Coalition Behaviour* (1970); G. Almond *et al.*, *Crisis, Choice, and Change* (1973); B. Barry, review article, *British Journal of Political Science* 7, Pt. II (Apr 1977) pp. 217—54.

2. See S. E. Finer (ed.), *Adversary Politics and Electoral Reform* (1975); D. Rae, *The Political Consequences of Electoral Laws* (1967); S. Rokkan and S. Lipset, *Party Systems and Voter Alignments* (1967); L. Dodd, *Coalitions in Parliamentary Government* (1976). See also P. Pulzer, 'Will Britain Lose Coalitions?', *Parliamentary Affairs*, **30**, 1 (1977), pp. 69—79 and M. Laver, 'Coalitions in Britain?', ibid, pp. 107–11.

# Index